Comprehensive
ANGER
MANAGEMENT

A Step-By-Step Guide To Transforming Your Anger

GENE MONTERASTELLI

Disclaimer

Tapping and EFT are new protocols and there is still much to be learned. This book is intended as information only. It is not capable of diagnosis and should not replace emotional, psychological, and/or medical care. Before you add anything new to your life including diet, exercise, or tapping, please consult your primary care physician.

ISBN 978-0-615-77702-3
Printed In The USA
Brother Blue Publishing

About The Author

Gene Monterastelli is the editor of Tapping Q & A and the host of the Tapping Q & A Podcast. He is an EFT practitioner based in Baltimore, Maryland who specializes in helping his clients to stop self-sabotaging and to reach their goals in physical fitness and weight, relationships, and work. Gene's favorite part of his week is teaching tapping to inmates as part of an advanced anger management class in a county jail.

Thank You And Appreciation

This book is the product of many people's time, effort, and resources.

First, I would like to thank all the guys who have shown up for class over the last two years. This book is based on the work of the "Advanced Anger Management Class" I teach in a local correctional facility. The class is not court ordered. Participants choose to be there because they have recognized that anger is an issue in their lives. Not only is their anger holding them back, but if they don't make a change they know it will get much worse. They have been some of the best teachers I have ever had. They are honest about where they are and truly want a better life.

Second, I would like thank Joyce Rader. Joyce works in the facility every day and her work is heroic. She works with and fights for men and women whom most people would simply dismiss. All the time she reminds the guys how much she cares for them. Joyce has courage and one of the biggest hearts of anyone I have ever met. Joyce is my hero!

In addition to Joyce I would like to thank Ron Ball, Tracy Middleton, and Anita Bains who taught the class before me. My work was only possible because of the amazing work they did.

Third, I would like to thank my editor Heidi Sheppard. She is so much more than an editor. In addition to making sure everything was grammatically correct she made sure this book was really good. She cared about the content as well as the form. On more than one occasion she gently reminded me to keep working and kept pushing me on. There is no way this book would exist without her effort and care.

Fourth, I would like to thank Gene and Rox Monterastelli. I would not do the work I do or be the person I am without their model.

We live in amazing times. Because of technology we are able connect to people all over the world. This book was championed by and invested in by people in Australia, Belgium, Canada, China, Iceland, Ireland, Mexico, the Netherlands, New Zealand, Switzerland, Turkey, the United Kingdom, and the United States. During the funding process I would tell the guys on the inside about your support. They spend a lot of time feeling forgotten and were stunned by the fact that people from all over the world wanted better for them.

The primary backers were: Jim Blue, Pamela Bruner, Jeff Hedglen, Carol Look, Mark 5:11 Ministries, Chris Padget, Jessica Ortner, Joyce Rader, Heidi Sheppard, Rod Sherwin, Ronald Shonk, Jason Strand, and Kate Walser.

Additionally this book could not have happened without the support of: Aila Accad, Anthony Albence, Stephen Barr, Sharon Bosmoore, Andy Bryce, Marilyn Buchanan, Lee Carter, Mike Corata, Katie Cornell, Brad and Joia Farmer, Jerry Goebel, Rue Hass, Natalie Hill, Marilyn Kinman, Valerie Lis, Mark Pasenoe, Jon Pressimone, Veronique Rooney, Catherine Simmons, Shelagh Smith, Jenny Stamm, Margaret Sutherland, Sue Tanida, Teri Terrusa, Laura Wallerstedt, Steve Wells, Jondi Whitis, and Brad Yates.

There were also many other contributors who chose to remain anonymous who have been thanked personally.

If you know of a facility that would be interested in this resource please feel free to contact me at gene@tappingqanda.com.

Chapter 1 – Introduction

Where This Book Came From And How It Changed Me

Since February of 2011 I have been blessed to be spending my Monday and Wednesday mornings in the local county jail helping out with the Advanced Anger Management class. It has been an amazing experience which has provided the inspiration for this book.

Recently I ran into my friend whose place I have taken as assistant teacher for the class. She asked, "Isn't it addictive?" Addictive is the only way I can describe it. It is one of the coolest things I have going on in my life right now.

In this book I will share with you the tools I teach my guys and I will show you exactly how to use them. Many of the tools include step-by-step instructions that only require you to follow along to unlock their power.

Before we dive into an understanding of anger, why we struggle with it, and how we can transform it, I want to share a little bit about what I have learned from the experience of teaching the class.

I have learned so much from the class. These lessons are not limited to how best to use or teach tapping, but I have also learned lots of lessons about life. By first understanding these lessons it will make it easier for you to access the tools in this book.

Here are ten lessons that I learned from teaching tapping in jail:

Choice

One of my favorite things about the class is the fact that it has not been court-ordered. Everyone is in the class by choice. I will admit that a few of the guys show up because they receive a certificate of participation for their file upon completion, but even these guys fully participate.

There is no mystery about what is going on. These guys recognize that because of their anger they have made choices that have created negative outcomes and they want to change this. Sometimes they are trying to change just to avoid negative outcomes while other times they are trying to change in order to be better people overall.

Regardless of why they are in class, it is their choice. Because of this openness we are willing to push them and challenge them to look very honestly at their lives, their past choices, and their beliefs about themselves. Sometimes this is a little work, but we all need to be pushed a bit to be honest with ourselves.

Lesson 1: *Healing and transformation will not take place unless it is a choice. We can't force someone to change. We can encourage people to change and we can support people in their change work, but we cannot force someone else to change.*

Safe Space

I am in awe of the woman who runs the class. She works for the county and is the one who is in charge of this class, as well as many others types of classes. She spends five days a week working inside an extremely restrictive environment trying to make the lives of a very marginalized population (both male and female) better. In her words and, more importantly, in her actions she shows how much she cares for the guys in class.

One of the main reasons the class works is because it feels like a safe space. The guys know they can talk about their issues and worries without fear of judgment or of negative repercussions. This safe and loving space exists because of the safe space that has been created with her heart.

One day the guys were asking if I am paid to teach the class. I told them I am a volunteer. When they asked the teacher the same questions she responded, "Yes, but they don't pay me to care." There are lots of people who the guys interact with in the facility who don't care. She does, and it makes all the difference.

Lesson 2: *It is important that the people we are working with understand that we care about them and that they are in a safe space when we work with them. Doing change work can be hard. Often we have to admit the things we don't like about ourselves. Creating a loving and safe environment makes it easier for them to choose the steps to healing.*

Other People's Emotions

We spend a great deal of time in class working with the guys' emotions about their relationships. These emotions fall into three basic categories. First, there are the relationships that are contentious. These are normally relationships with the mothers of their children. Second, there are the relationships where they feel like they have let others down. The guys are seeing firsthand how their choices are affecting others like their parents, their partners, and their children. It is really hard to see how our choices negatively impact others. Finally, there are emotions about the relationships in which they feel helpless. Because they are incarcerated the guys can't be helpful to their family members who are struggling with other personal problems.

As the guys have limited interaction with their loved ones (telephone, letters and occasional visits), it puts what they can and can't control into stark relief. When we are around someone frequently, I think we misunderstand how much influence we have over someone else's life. When we don't have much contact with them, it becomes much more obvious just how little influence we really have.

Because of this, we help the guys to spend a great deal of time talking about and tapping for what they do have control over, which is their own emotions. (The tool we use the most is "About... To...As if..." which we will cover in Part 5 of this book.)

Lesson 3: *In the end the only thing we control is our emotional response and our choices. We can't control other people's choices or their emotions nor are we responsible for other people's choices or emotions. When we stop spending time and energy trying to change the emotions of others we can direct our energy to the place we have the most control: inside ourselves.*

Twice A Week, Every Week

It is easy to pick out specific moments about the class to rave about. There are moments where there are amazing breakthroughs. There are great unplanned conversations about life where the guys wrestle with the really tough questions. As wonderful as these moments are they don't happen all class long and they don't even happen in every class. There are classes that feel long. There are times where the guys look at me bored, because I am sure they are bored with me.

Even though each class isn't amazing they create a cumulative effect. By being there twice a week every week, it helps to build a relationship. The more we show up, the more the guys trust us and trust the tool set. Sometimes it takes weeks before one of the guys will open up in class, but it is because of the constant contact and relationship that the opening up eventually happens.

Lesson 4: *Not everyone will trust us and start tapping right away. Sometimes we have to prove ourselves and our commitment to them over time. This does not mean that we run people over with our care, but it is important that we demonstrate that we are there for the long haul.*

What is that word?

Recently I brought to class a list of emotions that was created by The Center for Nonviolent Communication (which we will learn how to use in Part 5). The goal of the list is to help the guys develop a more specific vocabulary in describing how they feel. The more specifically we can describe how we feel, the easier it is to change how we feel.

When printed, the list is two pages long. After I handed out the list to the guys I started to explain why I had given them the list. As I was finishing "K" just blurted out, "What does this word mean?" He then asked about another and another and another. K is in his late thirties and is comfortable enough in his own skin that he wasn't concerned what I (or his classmates) thought about the fact he didn't understand something. His learning was more important than that.

I wish I could always approach learning in the same way.

Lesson 5: *It is OK to admit that we don't have all the answers and it is important to let others know that it is OK to ask for clarification when needed. If we remain in the dark we will not learn and we will often feel stupid because we don't know, which in turn shuts down the learning and/or healing process.*

Filling The Tool Box

There are lots of reasons why guys don't make it to class. It could be the unit's day to go to the library, they could be meeting with their lawyer, they could be in court, or something could have happened overnight and their unit is in lockdown so that no one can leave for any reason.

Because of this reality it is hard to teach concepts that build upon previous work because you never know who is going to be there and which classes they have already attended. To combat this I have broken down all the topics down into discrete parts. Each part contains two pieces: a tool that can be used right now and an explanation of how it fits into the big picture.

Ten Steps To Tap For Any Emotion (which you will learn in Part 5) is a perfect example of this approach that I created for class. If you know the tapping points and follow the steps, you will find relief. When working with the guys I presented the steps one at a time and had them write out their answers for each step.

After they completed the whole process we spent some time talking about how and why the process worked. We talked about the importance of each step and how it impacted the overall results.

In the end it didn't matter if they understood any of the big picture stuff. Of course understanding the big picture makes using and customizing the tools easier, but if the tools are understood and used regularly they will bring healing, and that is what is most important.

Lesson 6: *Don't give people concepts and theory. Give them tools they can use right now to improve their lives. If they are interested in theory they will ask about it. It is more important for someone to regain control of their life than it is for them to be able explain what is happening on an energetic level when someone is experiencing psychological reversal. This book is put together in such a way that you don't have to understand any of the concepts to be successful. If you work the steps you will see change.*

Class Time

Because of the nature of the facility it is hard to get the guys to class. They come from as many as ten different units, many of the inmates are not allowed to move through the facility on their own, class lists need to be submitted ahead of time, keys need to be checked out by officers, and the classroom has to be unlocked. There are an amazing number of moving parts and because of this we have two hour classes twice a week. This is so we can get a maximum amount of time in class with the least amount of disruption to the facility.

To be honest, two hours is a really difficult length of time in which to teach. It is just a little too long to go straight through and it is too short to take a break. It can be hard to hold the guys' attention and sometimes I find it hard to keep my energy up as a teacher for two straight hours. Also, the class is at 8:30 am so many of the guys have just rolled out of bed and aren't yet fully awake.

Lesson 7: *When you are doing this type of work it is important that you don't try to do too much at once. It is best to set aside a time each day to do this work instead of trying to do everything in one go. If you teaching this type of class it is important that when planning your material you keep in mind how long people can stay focused, how long you can teach, and the energy level of the room based on what has come right before class. If you are going to be teaching for a large chunk of time, switch from direct teaching/lecturing to providing experiential/hands-on activities in order to keep everyone focused and energized.*

Breathe In And Hold

Tapping in public can be a little bit embarrassing. Let's be honest, it does look rather silly. You can only imagine how much harder it must be to tap in jail! There is no privacy, your reputation can be very important, and you definitely don't want to look foolish.

At the beginning of one of the classes I asked the guys how it was going and if they were tapping back in the unit on their own. One of the guys said that he wasn't tapping, but he tried one of the "breathing thingies." (At the beginning or the end of most of the classes we do a guided imagery or breathing exercise. He was referring to one of these.)

He said that he was having a really hard time falling asleep because the jail is never quiet. There is always someone talking or something banging. Not being able to fall asleep really agitates him. He said that doing one of the breathing exercises calmed him enough to fall asleep. He then apologized for not tapping.

I told him that it didn't matter if he tapped or not. What was most important is he recognized what was going on, reached for a tool that he thought might work for him, and then used it. That was all I could ever ask for.

Lesson 8: *It is always about doing what makes sense and is useful. It is never about the toolset. I would love it if everyone in the world learned to tap, but I would love it even more if everyone were willing to take responsibility for their own healing and do something about it. It is easy for us to get wrapped up in getting people to tap because it has been so effective for us. We shouldn't let our love of the tool get in the way of other* *people's healing. When working through this book you will find things that work for you and things that don't. Do the ones that work for you.*

If You Have Time In Your Busy Schedule

One day in class I was introducing a tool that would take less than ten minutes to work through. I turned to the guys and said, "Sometime in the next 48 hours I would appreciate it if you could find some time in your busy schedule to carve out five or ten minutes to try this on your own." They all looked at me stunned and then broke out laughing.

Lesson 9: *It is good to be honest about where you are. It is not a mystery that the guys are in jail, that they have limited freedom, and are wearing colored jumpsuits for a reason. They know they are in jail. I know they are in jail. Being honest about where we are and what is going on gives us the greatest chance for healing. As you engage in the tools in this book remember you are not being graded and no one will see your answers. This is about you and your healing. The more honest you are about what is going on, the more likely it is that you will effect change and transformation.*

Lesson 10: *Just because something is grave doesn't mean it has to be serious all the time. There are lots of things that are both serious and important, but I have found in my own life that if I lose my sense of humor in the serious moments I am more likely to feel overwhelmed. It is ok for us to laugh. Gallows humor can be very helpful and healing. Don't be afraid to joke about what you are going through. There are times where joking about how far you need to go will help your healing process.*

Let's Begin

As I said before, I have used the tools in the book many times to help guys who are seeing the choices they made in anger harm their lives in big ways. Many of them have undergone radical transformation because they have been willing to do the work and work through the steps.

Reading this book will not be enough. Understanding the concepts in this book will not be enough. If you want change, if you want to stop being controlled by your anger, then you will need to work through the steps. Be honest, be open, and this will help you to be free.

What Is Anger And Why Do We Need It?

Because you have picked up this book I am going to assume you have an issue with anger, otherwise you wouldn't be trying to manage it. Most of the people I have worked with on anger management just want it to go away. It is a force in their lives that takes over everything when it rises up. One of my students would always talk about his anger as "the dragon." It was something that came out of nowhere, completely took over when it arrived, and when it was spent almost felt like an out-of-body experience.

Whoever came up with the comic book character The Incredible Hulk truly understood the uncontrolled power of anger and rage.

The goal of this book is not to eliminate anger from your life. Anger is useful. We need anger. The problem comes when it is showing up too often or disproportionately in a given situation.

It Is All Information

Our system is an information system. What I mean by that is that everything that we experience in our bodies is information to help us make choices.

The information communicated by anger is that we are under attack and we need to protect ourselves. At first, that might not seem right because most of the time when we feel anger we aren't really under attack. And that is part of the problem. When we get to the point where we have a problem with our anger it is because it is showing up more forcefully than necessary, or at times when we aren't really under attack.

Anger Is Not The Problem

With this understanding we can see how anger can be good for us and helps us to stay safe. When someone comes at me with a knife it is a good thing that I get a surge of strength and energy to help me to protect myself. It is a good thing that when I am cut off in traffic a rush of energy helps me to grip the steering wheel and quickly focus my vision so that I can control the car safely.

The problem comes when someone disagrees with me over the price of something and my system perceives that as an attack and my anger shows up to fight back. The problem is when the waiter messes up my order and I get mad and throw the food back in his face. The problem is when the phone doesn't work and I throw it against the wall.

In all of these cases there is a part of me that has wrongly perceived what has happened as an attack.

In this process the aim is not to stop you from being able to feel anger. The aim is to help you move to a place where anger only appears when it is needed and only to the degree that it is useful.

What Does Success Look Like?

Before we begin any sort of work it is important that we have a clear sense of what success looks like when it comes to changing how and when we feel anger. When we are working towards managing our anger it is not as simple as one day we feel anger and the next day we don't. As we just talked about, anger itself is not the enemy. Anger is a useful emotion when it shows up at the right time and to the right degree.

As we work through this process there will be four very clear ways of knowing that we are having success and making progress.

1) Name what has caused us problems in the past

The fact that you are trying to do something about your anger shows that you know it is an issue for you and more than likely you can describe in great detail the times your anger has gotten the best of you. But we need to do more than just recognize that it is there, we need to understand what has happened in the past and why.

When we have done this we will be able to see patterns to our choices and find root causes for why we acted in a particular way. When we see past events more clearly for what they are, we can use this information to aid the healing process.

It is not always easy to dig back into our past to look at the poor choices we made and how those choices have impacted our loved ones. Even though it isn't enjoyable it is important work.

We will know we are making progress towards managing our anger when we can clearly state what has caused us to experience extreme anger in the past.

2) Name the situations that cause us problems now and come up with strategies to manage them more effectively

There are people, places, and situations that are hard for us every time we encounter them. When we are able to name the people who push our buttons and the situations that drive us crazy, and why they give us trouble, we are able to approach them in new ways so that they are much less likely to get the better of us.

In this process we will name the exact situations that push our buttons and come up with very specific plans to respond in a better way. By having a clear sense of where the problem spots are and how we can respond, we will be able to make better choices and much less likely to be consumed with anger.

3) Name difficulties as they are happening

Often when we respond in anger it happens in an unconscious and sudden way. One moment we are fine, the next we are caught up in rage. When we are able to name the situations that cause us anger, we are able to see them unfold as they happen. When this happens we can respond differently in the moment to slow the anger down.

Through this process you will learn how to slow the moment down to the point where you can feel the anger building up. As the anger is building up you will be able to choose a reaction that is free from excessive anger.

4) Become more skilled at describing what happened

There is a big difference in recognizing "I got really angry," and "I got really angry because I thought that they were trying to take advantage of me." The more time we spend thinking about and understanding why we respond in anger, the better we will become at understanding future moments of anger. This understanding will in turn allow us to leave the state of anger, and will make us less likely to be angry in the same way in future.

This Book

Each of the tools in this book uses at least one of these approaches. Many of the tools will use more than one. It is important that we approach our anger from a number of different angles. This will help us to heal past issues, give us tools to respond to what is happening in the moment, and to learn from each new situation.

To that end make sure you do all the tools in the book as they work together. By taking this multifaceted approach we give ourselves the best chance of long-term, lasting success.

Chapter 2 –
Where To Start

Naming Our Goals When We Start

When I am teaching these tools in class the first thing we do is have everyone introduce themselves. During the introduction everyone is asked to share three things: their name, what they have gained in past anger management classes (if they have taken any), and what they hope to achieve with this class. Of those three things, the third is the most important in setting the class up for success

What Change Do You Want AND Why Do You Want It?
Whenever we try to achieve something new it is important to name what we are seeking. The more specifically we are able to name our goal, the easier it will be for us to achieve it. Take getting healthy for example. Our goal could be:

- I want to get in shape
- I want to lose 25 pounds
- I want to run a half marathon in March of next year

As the goal becomes more specific, the easier it is to create a plan for achieving it. The goal "I want to get into shape" means I need to do some exercise, but when I say "I want run a half marathon" this focuses the type of exercise and training required.

Creating Goals
When we are looking to manage our anger we need a clear vision of what we want to make it easier to move towards our goal. We will create our goal in three steps:

- What do I want?
- Why do I want it?
- How will I know I have achieved it?

Let's look at these one at a time.

What Do I Want?

As stated above, the key to creating useful and motivating goals is to be specific. To do this, describe what you are trying to achieve in as much detail as possible. As you describe your goal imagine you are being asked questions by a small child. Small children never to seem run out of questions. They will keep asking, "What do you mean by that?"

When you are creating your goal ask yourself questions over again and again. For example:

Goal: I want to get my anger under control

Q: What do you mean by "under control"?

Goal: I want to get my anger under control so it doesn't consume me.

Q: What do you mean by "consume me"?

Goal: I want to get my anger under control to the point that when I encounter something that makes me mad I am able to respond in a reasonable and rational way.

You can continue this process as long as you need to. The more detail better.

Why do you want this?

For me this is the most important part of any goal that we create. It is easy to lose our attachment to a goal because it is something that isn't yet real, but there is often a lot of emotion around why we want something. Below is a real world example to show you how this works.

I was working with "Chris" to lose weight. He had gained and lost over 150 lbs in his life. He would lose 30 lbs and then slowly gain it back. He did this over and over again. His doctor was getting concerned. He told Chris, "This has to stop. Not only is losing and regaining the weight really hard on your body, your family history is working against you. You know that heart disease runs in families. If you don't lose and keep the weight off you will be in trouble. Tell me the truth, do you want to see your daughter get married?"

Chris said of course he did. His daughter was only six years old, but it was something every father dreams of.

His doctor said, "Then you have to change! If you don't lose this weight and keep it off you will not live to walk your daughter down the aisle!"

In that moment losing weight and getting in shape went from something that seemed like a good idea to something that was really, really important.

Because Chris knew why he wanted to lose the weight it was much easier to stay motivated. To keep this in the front of his mind he took his six year old daughter to a bridal shop. He dressed her in an adult wedding dress. She was cute as can be swimming in satin and lace. Chris took a bunch of photos. He posted one on the fridge at home, one on the fridge at work, and put one in his wallet. Every time he was tempted to snack between meals he would see the photo of his daughter in that wedding dress and it would remind of him why he needed to make better choices.

This didn't mean that he made better choices every time, but it did help him tap into the motivation to make better choices.

When we create a goal of any type it is important to understand why we want it to help us stay focused, for example:

- I want to get my anger under control so that I don't yell all the time and make my daughter scared to be around me.
- I want to get my anger under control so that I don't lash out in physical rage which lands me in trouble.
- I want to get my anger under control so that I don't drink all the time to numb the feeling of constant rage.

How will I know when I have achieved by goal?

Finally, it is important for us to be able to measure our progress to make sure that we are moving forward and getting closer to our goal. Sometime this is easy to do because of the nature of the goal we are trying to achieve, such as losing 25 lb or being able to run 5 km without stopping.

Other goals can be more difficult to measure. When we are working towards something that can't be easily measured we need to come up with a list of outcomes that show we are moving towards achieving our goal.
For example:

Goal: I want to be less depressed and happier.
How I can tell: In the evening instead of sitting on the couch watching hours of TV and eating mindlessly I go for a walk and/or talk to friends.

Goal: I want to get my anger under control.

How I can tell: When I disagree with someone I state why I disagree instead of yelling at them.

Conclusion

When we are able to state what we want, why we want it, and what success looks like, it will help us to move towards our goal.

To that end take some time to do exactly that right now.

1) What do you want? (Provide as much detail as possible.)

2) Why do you want it? (Name at least 5 reasons you want this.)

3) How will you know you have achieved this? (Name at least 3 positive outcomes to achieving this goal.)

What Did You Achieve In The Past?

There is a lot to be said for celebrating successes, even if they are small. Research has shown that this is a great motivator for making better choices in the future. This is also true for other people's success. When we see other people being successful we think, "They did this, so I can too!"

Normally we don't notice our successes. We usually notice and remember the things that didn't go as planned. On one level this makes sense. We do this to see what we can correct and/or we do this to beat ourselves up for the things we have done wrong.

What we don't normally do is spend much time thinking about what has gone well. Take driving a car as an example. When you think of your experience as a driver you can remember the number of accidents you have been in fairly easily. I know I can vividly remember an accident I was in back in 1986. What we don't give a great deal of thought to is all the times we arrived somewhere safely. In the last few months I have driven well over one hundred times and I can tell you none of the details of any of those safe journeys.

When we are trying to change something about ourselves it is helpful for us to spend a little time thinking about how we have made progress in the past. Even if it isn't in this area of our lives, if we can notice a change we have made before in another area of our lives it can serve as motivation to make change in our current area of focus.

Take a few moments to answer the following:

1) In the past how have I changed something in my life? And what are some of the good choices I have made in this area of my life?

2) Which other areas of my life have I wanted to change and I was able to do so?

3) Who do I know has already made the type of change that I am wanting to make? (If you don't know anyone personally do some research to find people who have made the change that you want to make.)

Anger Management Pre-Test

It is important for us to have a baseline from which to work. This will be helpful in two ways. First, it will help us to see the progress have made after we have worked through the tools in this book. Second, by asking questions about the different ways we experience anger it will help us to understand what we are working with more clearly.

The statements below describe situations that you may have experienced in your day-to-day life. If you haven't experienced a situation just try to imagine how you might react. Use the scoring scale to identify the response you are most likely to have in that scenario and write your score for each statement in the space provided. Take the time you need to decide, but keep in mind that your first reaction is generally the most accurate.

3 for "often"; 2 for "some of the time"; 1 for "rarely"; 0 for "never"

_____ I think that other people cause me to be angry.

_____ When someone disagrees with me, I work hard to make sure they know that they're wrong.

_____ When I think about something that bothered me in the past, I can get very angry about it all over again.

_____ I think that people who make mistakes should be reprimanded and clearly told they did something wrong.

_____ I feel impatient when I have to wait in a line.

_____ When I am around people I don't like, I let them know in one way or another.

_____ When I see someone who is overweight, I start to think about how little self-discipline he or she has.

_____ When I get really angry I throw, hit, or break things.

_____ I get angry if things don't go the way I want them to go.

_____ When something does not go my way, I progress from having no anger to experiencing rage and aggression in seconds.

_____ I get really upset with myself when I make a mistake or don't do something well.

_____ When someone treats me badly, I start to think about ways to get even with them.

_____ If I'm really mad at other people, I'm likely to put them down and swear at them.

_____ I generally believe that people would be dishonest if they could actually get away with it.

_____ My anger overwhelms me at times and I seem to lose control.

_____ If someone hurts or offends me, I end up thinking about it a lot and have a hard time letting it go.

_____ When I get angry, I've experienced chest pain, headaches, or other physical symptoms.

_____ When I have something important to say I want to jump in and interrupt other people, rather than listen.

_____ Other people tell me they are worried and tell me about what happens when I get angry or how often I get mad.

_____ I don't like how I behave when I get angry and I end up feeling bad about what I said or did.

_____ I think I have a "thin skin" and am easily affected by what others say and do.

Total up your score.

(Adapted from Tracey Middleton's adaptation of work of David J. Decker, MA, LP.)

Chapter 3 –
Tapping

What Is Tapping?

Many of tools in this book will use something that I simply refer to as "tapping". There are many different ways to do tapping. The very first version was developed by Dr. Roger Callahan and he called it Thought Field Therapy. In later years, building on the work of Dr. Callahan, Gary Craig developed a simpler version that he called Emotional Freedom Techniques (EFT).

Since then a number of versions and variations have been created. Personally, I view many of the newer versions of tapping to be much like the older ones with the only real difference being the name or the order in which you do things.

To that end I am simply going to refer to what we will be doing as tapping.

Basics Of Tapping

The way I approach tapping is with the following formula: tapping + tuning into issue = relief.

The tapping part is very simple. We will use 9 points on the body.

[A drawing of the tapping points can be found on page 34]

KC (Karate Chop): This point is on the side of the hand, the part that you would use if you were going to break a board with a karate chop. Use the fingertips of all four fingers of one hand to tap on the fleshy part of the side of the other hand.

TH (Top of the Head): This is located on the very tippy top of your head. The place to tap is the space where the piece of metal hits the top of your head when the doctor is measuring your height. Please note that this point can be very tender because you are tapping right on top of your brain. If it hurts to tap here just tap a few inches above the head without making contact.

EB (Eyebrow): When you tap on the eyebrow tap as far to the inside of the eyebrow without falling down onto the nose, using two fingers.

SE (Side of the Eye): This tapping point is located on the edge of your eye socket. Make sure you are on the ridge outside the eye, without touching your eyeball or eyelid. Use two fingers on this tapping point.

UE (Under the Eye): This point is on your cheek, directly below the iris of your eye. Use two fingers to tap on this point. There is a sinus cavity directly under this point so if you find it too tender to tap you can lightly touch the point and rub in small circles.

UN (Under the Nose): Use two fingers on this point which is located directly below the nose and above the upper lip.

C (Chin): The tapping point is located halfway between the point of your chin and your lower lip. Use two fingers on this tapping point.

CB (Collar Bone): This tapping point is located just under the collar bone near the center of the chest. To tap on this point use your whole hand. You can use either hand. I am going to use the right hand for the explanation, but you can use either. Open your right hand so you are looking at the palm of a flat hand. As you lay your hand flat on your chest place your right thumb along the right collar bone and lay your right index finger on the left collar bone. Use the whole hand and pat your chest like you were burping a baby.

UA (Under the Arm): Use all four fingertips to tap on the point located under your arm, located in the middle, as you move from front to back on your side. The point is about bra strap height. The place you tap will feel a bit like a bruise. You can tap on this point by reaching across your body or you can tap under the arm you are using to tap. If you don't feel confident that you are tapping on the right spot, just tap the entire area.

Notes On Tapping

With each of the tools in this book you will be answering questions or saying phrases out loud and tapping on your body using the points I just described. You will move from tapping point to tapping point as you follow the instructions in each tool.

As we move through the process this is going to make more sense, but for now here are the basics.

How many times do I tap?
Tap on each spot six to eight times. Often you will be tapping while you are reading a script. If you are doing this you will tap on each point while you read one sentence. When you reach the end of sentence, move on to the next tapping point.

Which hand should I tap with?
It doesn't matter which hand you use to tap. You will also notice that many of the tapping points can be found on both sides of the body. You can tap on either point with either hand. For example, you can use your right hand and tap on the right or left eyebrow and receive the same benefit. Some people like to use both hands when tapping, for example tapping with the right hand on the right eyebrow and the left hand of the left eyebrow.

Should I tap in a specific order?
The order you tap in is not important. The points above were explained in the order that the points line up neatly on the body. You can tap on the points in any order you want. It is most common to tap through them in the order above, but do what is most comfortable.

What if I am not sure if I am getting the right spot?
The nice thing about tapping is that it is a very forgiving tool. You just need it to be close. If you don't feel you are getting the point exactly right just tap in a small circle covering as much of the area as possible. Nothing bad can happen if you tap on the wrong spot (assuming you are not poking your eyes out).

What happens if it hurts when I tap somewhere?
STOP! Tapping should not be painful. You need to take total responsibility for yourself when tapping. If it hurts beyond mild tenderness, don't do it. If one of the tapping points hurts then just rub it. If it hurts to rub it, just touch the point and take deep breaths.

Tuning In

Now that you have a little bit of a sense of how to tap on your body, the second and most important part of tapping is the tuning in or paying attention to the issue at hand. The more detail we have and the more focused we are on an issue, the more effective tapping will be. Most of this book is dedicated to giving you tools to do just that. I will give you a brief example of how easy it is to tune in so that you understand the concept, but after that you don't need to give it much thought because this book provides you with all the tools you need to tune in.

When I say "tuning in" all I mean is giving your conscious attention to something. For example, I want you to think about your shoes and how they are touching your feet. As you read that line and gave your feet some thought you had one of two experiences. Either you are wearing shoes and/or socks and you felt them touching your feet, or you aren't wearing anything on your feet and you noticed how free your feet feel.

Either way, before reading the line of instructions you weren't thinking about your feet at all. When you thought of your feet you could feel whatever was on them. Socks didn't magically appear on your feet when you thought of them, you were just tuning that piece of information out. By giving them a little attention you noticed what was always there.

We are able to tune in and out of most things. You could have a sore knee which you don't notice during the day, but when you sit down, take a deep breath and relax, all of sudden you start to notice the aching. Your knee didn't begin to ache when you sat down, but you tuned it out during the day and now that you are not doing anything else you tune back into the pain.

We are able to tune in and out of things besides physical sensations. When we are sitting in the middle of a busy restaurant with lots of people talking we are able tune out everyone else and focus on the person we are talking to. We can watch a sporting event or movie and completely lose connection with everything else in the world.

When we are tapping we want to give as much attention as possible to the issue at hand. The more focused we are on what is going on, the more powerful the tapping will be. To show you how easy it is to tune into something in a more specific way there are a series of statements below. I don't want to you read them all once. Read the first statement and take a moment to do what it says. After you have given it 10 to 15 seconds move on to the next statement.

- Imagine one of the classrooms you attended in 2nd, 3rd, or 4th grade
- Imagine what your teacher looked like
- Imagine what your desk looked like

- Imagine some of the kids who sat around you or were friends at the time
- Imagine what is on the walls of the classroom

As you read some of the statements you remembered lots of details while it might have been harder to get an image for others. As you moved from statement to statement the classroom became increasingly clear. After the first statement you were tuned into the classroom, but by the fifth statement you were even more focused.

Whatever you are tapping on, the more tuned into the issue you want to address, the more effective the tapping will be.

I know this sounds like a lot to begin with. This book is written so that you don't have to worry about any of this. All you need to do is know where the tapping points are, follow the instructions for each of the tools, and tap. If you do that, even if you don't understand a single thing about the tapping itself, you will find relief.

A Few More Thoughts On Tapping

It looks weird! It feels weird!

Yes, tapping looks very weird. Yes, tapping feels very weird. There are lots of things that we do today that would have seem very strange to generations that came before us. At a certain point getting better becomes more important than how it looks or feels. In the next section I will talk about how to tap in a discrete way so that other people don't see you doing it. In the meantime, it is OK to accept the fact that it is odd.

I don't believe it will work!

I know. It seems unbelievable that you should be able to tap on your body in this seemingly random way and find some relief. I feel that way sometimes myself. I have done this professionally for years and there are things that I have experienced that still seem impossible.

One of the best parts about tapping is that you don't need to believe that it will work for it to work. In that way, it is kind of like aspirin. It doesn't matter if you believe an aspirin is going to help your headache when you take it, it will work regardless.

If you carefully follow the steps in the book it will make a big difference. It doesn't matter if you believe it or not. The important thing is you have to give it an honest effort. If you only answer half of the questions in one of the tools and try tapping for 15 seconds you will not be successful. Your failure will be due to your lack of effort, not because the tool failed you.

Step into this with an open mind. Each of the exercises is designed to help you understand yourself a little better. If you give this an honest try it will make a difference.

Tapping For Something Physical

As an introduction to using tapping we will start by giving it a try by tapping on a physical ache or pain. We are going to do this for two reasons.

First, it will be a simple introduction to the technique, with the added benefit of showing you how to take care of physical pain with tapping. Second, physical pain can impact our emotional state. When we are in pain (like when we have a headache) we can be much crankier and more likely to get angry. When we tap for physical aches and pains we help ourselves to make fewer emotional choices.

To do this we are going to follow three simple steps.

1) Choose a physical pain to tap for

If nothing comes to mind right away, take a deep breath and scan your body for something. For each of the following questions I want you to write down your answer as we are going to use your answers in the next step.

- Where is the pain located? Be as specific as possible when describing the location. For example don't write "my right knee" but "on the front of my right knee on the knee cap." The more specific the better.
- What type of pain is it? Is it dull, sharp, achy, pulsing, itchy, or hot? The more detailed the description the better.
- What is the Subject Unit of Distress Scale (SUDS)? This is a rating from 0–10 of the pain. 0 is no pain at all and 10 is the worst pain you have ever felt. Don't get too hung up on coming up with exactly the right number.
- What is the 3D shape of the pain? Is it flat on the surface of the skin, does it feel like a ball of pain, is it a long strip of tightness that runs the length of the muscle, or does it have a round center with tentacles of pain spreading out in all directions? Again, the more detail you can provide the better.
- Is there an epicenter to the pain and where is it located? Is the pain evenly distributed? Does it have more than one center with the rest fanning out?
- How much does the pain weigh? If you were to guess and pretend that you could hold the pain in your hand, how much would it weigh? You don't need to know exact pounds, but does it weigh as much as a grapefruit, a steel rod, or is it as light as a feather?
- If you were to paint a picture of the pain to show to someone else what color or colors would you use? Be specific. Don't just write red. Is it fire truck red or rust red? Is it red in the middle and fading to light blues as you get to edge of the pain? Describe the color in as much detail as possible.

- If you were to make a model of this pain what material would you use to make it? Would it be a ball of hard rubber, burning lava, metal wire, or does it feel like a mass of cotton candy?
- Image a little cartoon face on the front of the pain. If it could talk, what would it say? It might say something specific, it might scream in pain, or it might just stick its tongue out at you. Give it a voice and what would it say?
- What does the pain remind you of? Just write the first thing that comes to mind. It could be a person, a place, or a situation.
- What emotion is associated with the pain? Again, don't give this a lot of thought, just the first thing that comes to mind.
- What memory is associated with the pain? There may not be one, but when you read that question, what is the first thing that came to mind?
- Is the pain associated with someone? Don't think about this too much, but who comes to mind and why?
- What does the pain need? Does it need to be heard? Does it need you to do something? Just ask the pain, what does it need, and write the answer down.
- What does the pain want you to learn? It might not want you to learn anything, but ask the pain what it needs.

2) Tap for the pain

Take all the answers you have written down and tap through them. With each new sentence move to a new tapping point. To do this start tapping on the first tapping point. Read the first question and as you read the answer concentrate on it. Once you have done this move to the second tapping point and repeat the process with the second question. When you have used up all the tapping points simply return to the first tapping point and work through them all again until you are out of questions.

3) Re-rate the pain level

After tapping though the list above rate the pain again on a scale of 0–10. If the pain has not reduced to a level that you are happy with, tap through steps 2 and 3 again.

It is really that simple. Before you move on I would encourage you to try tapping for something physical a few more times. This will give you a little more practice and a few different experiences of what tapping is like, making it easier as we add new things to the process.

Tapping For Any Negative Emotion

Now that you have had a chance to try tapping on something physical we are going to try tapping on something emotional. Tapping is a great tool to use for any negative emotion that we are feeling, not just anger.

Once again to make it easy I have created a simple step-by-step process for you to follow. As you are doing this make you have a piece of paper and write down the answer to each of the questions because we will use your answers in later steps.

1) Name The Emotion

This is very easy to do. I want you to think of an emotion that you have that you don't enjoy. This could be anger, sadness, overwhelm, stress, or frustration. We are going to be spending the bulk of our time in this book working with anger, but for this first experience of tapping for an emotion you don't have to choose anger.

2) Name A Specific Instance

In as much detail as you can come up with describe one specific instance of when you felt this emotion. Talk about who was there, what was said, what you were thinking, what you are thinking now as you remember it, and all the outcomes of the situation. Imagine you are sitting across from me in a coffee shop and telling me exactly what happened as if I know none of the details.

3) Rate The Emotion On The SUDS Scale

As you tune back into the story how big does the emotion feel? On a scale of 0–10 rate how strong the emotion is right now. 0 would be no emotion and 10 would be that you are totally consumed by the emotion.

4) Describe The Physical Sensations

In as much detail as possible describe the physical sensation(s) that go along with the emotion. In which part (or parts) of the body do you feel it? Is it hot, tight, heavy, itchy, stiff, or some other feeling? Does your face feel flushed, does your chest feel tight, or do you feel butterflies in your stomach? Do you feel it in more than one part of the body? Describe each part separately. Is there some sort of mental dialogue going on as you feel the emotion? What is the internal voice saying? Who does the voice sound like? Who does it remind you of?

5) List 3 Things That Went Wrong

Because of the instance you describe above what are (at least) three things that went wrong and how were/are you impacted by these outcomes? Sometimes one moment can impact later events and moments. Don't just think of what went wrong in the moment, but also how it impacted you later. Again, the more detail the better.

6) List 3 Outcomes You Would Like To Have Happened Instead

After something goes wrong there are ways we would have liked to have seen it turn out better. What are (at least) three hopes you have for the future? Is there a relationship you would like to mend? Is there something you would like someone to do? Is there a lesson you would like to learn? It is helpful to name how we would like things to turn out.

7) Re-rate On The SUDS Scale

After doing these steps I always like to re-rate the level of emotion. One of three outcomes are possible. First, the number could go up. This is because you have now spent time thinking about the issue in detail. Often this tunes us into the issue more sharply so that we notice it more, making it feel bigger.

Second, you may notice that the number goes down. Many times simply getting something out of your head will take the power out of it. Our minds can be relentless echo chambers, taking negative thoughts or emotions and just bouncing them around over and over again. When we drag them into the light of day they lose their intensity.

Finally, there might be no change at all. This simply means that more tapping is needed to shift the emotion.

8) Start To Tap

Go back to the top of your page and just start reading out loud what you have written. At the end of each sentence move to the next tapping point. This is not a race. There is no reason to rush. As you read the words out loud pay close attention to what you are saying. If you are describing what happened, re-live what you are saying. If you are talking about how you would like to see things turn out in the future really tune into the emotion of having the new and better outcome.

9) Take Notes While You Are Tapping

As you re-read what you have written it is possible that new details will come into focus. You might also notice new and even better possible outcomes around this issue for the future. If these things come to mind it is worthwhile taking the time to write them down. Not only will you learn things about this particular issue, but you will also learn things about yourself and the larger scope of this emotion.

10) Re-Rate One More Time

After you have read through what you have written and have tapped along, re-rate the issue to see where it is now. If you are down to a zero you are finished, if you are not (which is more likely) then you have the chance to move back to the top of page and tap again.

Hopefully you feel a little bit (or a lot) better. And yes, it feels really weird to tap on your body and have emotion release like that. Don't worry about what just happened or why it worked. Just trust the process. Remember the tools in this book are set up so that you don't have to know how things work, you just have to follow the steps.

Covert/Hidden Tapping

As we have already talked about, tapping is a little bit weird. AND it looks really weird.

There will be times when it will not feel comfortable to tap because we are in a public place. For tapping to work we need to be tuned into the issue we are working on in the moment. If we are worried about what others are thinking while we tap then we will not be successful.

There is an easy way around this. We can tap in such a way that it doesn't look like we are tapping at all. You already know how to do this. You have been doing this for years without realizing it because you were doing it out of habit and instinct.

Think about what happens when you are really tired, frustrated, or have a headache. You rub your temples, which is just like tapping the outside the eye point. Or you might take your glasses off and rub the bridge of your nose, which is the same thing as tapping on the eyebrow point. When I am thinking I take my index finger and line it under my nose like I am telling someone "shhhhh" and I tap my finger on my lips and chin, which is just like tapping under the nose and chin point all at once.

We were never taught to do these things. We do them because they bring us relief. Just like a baby is not taught to suck its thumb, it does it instinctively because it brings comfort.

When it comes to tapping in a covert way it is no different to normal tapping. The only difference is instead of openly tapping on each point before moving to the next one, we are hitting the points in a less obvious way.

For example, right now you could be working on one the exercises in this book, while you are reading through one of the tapping scripts you could reach up and rub the bridge of your nose, rub your temples, tap your index finger like you are saying "shhhh" and scratch your collarbone. Just like that you have hit five of the tapping points without anyone being the wiser.

It is also important to remember that you don't have to hit every single tapping point every time you are tapping. For me the collarbone point is particularly effective in finding relief. When I am sitting in public and something comes up that I want to tap on I will just take my hand and lay it flat across the top of my chest and gently start tapping. It might look a little odd, but the next time you are in a place where a bunch of people are reading or working quietly notice all the odd ways they are sitting. If you tap in this subtle way it will go unnoticed.

Tapping is such a powerful tool that we don't want to miss the opportunity to take advantage of using it because we are worried about what others think. By giving it a little thought we can tap in such a way that no one will be aware of what we are doing.

Chapter 4 –
The Process

Introduction To The Process

So far we have taken a look at what anger is, why we have it, and how to do the basics of tapping. In this part we will explore what anger is in much more detail, how it impacts our choices, and important concepts to keep in mind when working through any process to help manage anger.

As you become familiar with all these concepts you will gain a much better understanding of specifically why you feel anger. As we talked about in the "How Do We Know We Are Being Successful" section, when we have a better understanding of how and why we are responding to situations or people with anger, it will help us use the tools to respond better.

How Is It Working For You?

In this book you will find lots of resources. Many of them have multiple steps. Some of tools have different options on how to use them. As you use tapping and these tools you will find that some work for you better than others. The most important question to ask yourself is, "How is it working for me?"

The goal is not to memorize the tools so you don't need the book. The goal isn't to use the tools exactly and perfectly as they are described here. The goal of the book isn't for you to do every tool in this book over and over again.

The goal of this book is relief and healing. The goal of this book is to help you have a better understanding of your anger and be able to control it better.

As you use this book and work through the different tools you might ask:

- Do I need to tap on all the tapping points or can I just use a few of them?
- Do I need to say the phrases out loud or can I just think them in my mind?
- Do I need to do repeat every round of tapping as is described in a tool?
- Do I need to do every tool in this book?

To all of these questions I would answer, "How is it working for you?" If it is working, keep doing what you are doing. If it is not working, change something.

I need you to be very careful in the way that you hear and heed this advice. I am not saying that you should take the easy way out. There will be times where I ask you to do things or think of things that are uncomfortable. When we go through a healing process we will come into contact with things we don't like about ourselves, our lives, and painful choices from the past.

It would be easy to come across a part of your life that you don't like and think, "Gene said I didn't have to do all the steps, therefore I am going to skip this part here."

That is NOT what I am saying. The tools in this book are tried and true but you need to put forth an honest effort for them to work. Once you have tried the tools as listed two or three times feel free to change them if you are not getting the result that you want.

Remember, the goal is healing and transformation. This might mean that you will to need to change the tools to fit your specific needs, but when you change them you need to change them to be more useful, not just more comfortable.

The Three Minds

There are three parts to the human mind. There is the unconscious, the subconscious, and the conscious. Having a basic understanding about these parts of the mind will be very important in understanding how and why anger affects us, why it is so powerful, and how we can move to responses other than anger.

Don't worry. This isn't going to be super-complicated. You just need to understand the basic functions of each part of your mind.

The Unconscious Mind

I like to refer to the unconscious mind as the "lizard brain." The lizard brain is the oldest and most primitive part of our brain. We call tell how smart an animal is based on the size of its brain in comparison to the rest of its body. Humans have a very large brain in comparison to the size of our bodies.

Lizards on the other hand have very small brains. An alligator, for example, has a brain about the size of a lima bean and because of this they are only capable of primitive thoughts.

Our lizard brain is responsible for all the things that happen on an unconscious level. This is the part of the brain that is responsible for breathing, digestion, circulation, and growing new cells. Fortunately for us we don't have to spend time thinking, "breathe, breathe, breathe.... digest, digest, digest..." The lizard brain takes care of this for us.

The Subconscious Mind

I like to call the subconscious mind the "puppy brain." The reason I call it the puppy brain is because it reacts to the world in the same way a puppy does. A puppy thinks whatever is in front of it is the most important thing in the world. A puppy will see someone walking by and will jump up and bark. Then the puppy will see a falling leaf and will rush over to it as if it is the only thing in the world. Then it will hear someone approaching and rush to the back gate to see who it is, completely forgetting about the falling leaf.

The puppy brain holds all of our memories and all of our information about the world. When I am walking through the park and I see a giant green shaky thing I don't run away thinking it is a monster. My puppy brain recognizes that it is a tree. Even if I have never seen this type of tree before it will be able to tell it is a tree.

We don't have all of the information about the world and all of our memories at the front of our minds. It is all stored in the puppy brain. As we go through our day and encounter new things the puppy brain brings forward all the pertinent information.

For example, as I walk down the street I see someone walking towards me. The puppy brain quickly finds all the information that is associated with the person approaching. If it is someone I recognize it brings forward that information.

The puppy brain usually produces this information in what feels like an instant, but there are times where we can feel it taking longer. We see someone we know, but can't remember their name. We can almost feel ourselves searching our memory for their name and where we know them from.

The puppy brain keeps us safe

One of the characteristics of the puppy brain is that as it brings information forward it prioritizes information related to danger and in so doing drowns out all other information. For example, I am crossing the street and I look up to see a car. The puppy brain will bring the following information forward:

- Car
- Red
- Late 60s Mustang
- YOU ARE GOING TO DIE

I will react to the danger signal enabling me to jump out of the way to safety. It is a very good thing that the danger signal overrides everything else. The last thing I want to do in that situation is stand in the middle of the street admiring how well the owner has restored this classic car.

The puppy brain over-working

It is important to note that just because information is stored in the puppy brain it doesn't mean that it is accurate information. A perfect example of this is an irrational fear. For example, I am sitting at the kitchen table and on hearing a scratching sound, and I look over to the counter to see a mouse eating some crumbs. The puppy brain brings the following information forward:

- Little
- Grey
- Eats cheese
- Made Cinderella's dress
- YOU ARE GOING TO DIE

In an instant I jump up on the table and scream like a small child. The puppy brain is keeping me safe from the mouse in the same way it kept me safe from the car, but it was working from inaccurate information. Consciously I know that the mouse is not dangerous but the puppy brain automatically supplies information to the front of our minds because it thinks it is true.

The puppy brain is also the place where all of our emotions live. This is the main reason why becoming angry affects our emotional choices. When we are consumed by anger we act without stopping to think. After the fact we can see why this was a poor choice or an over-emotional choice but in the moment it just takes over.

Much of the work you will do in this book will be about making changes to the information in the puppy brain so it doesn't overreact or act on impulses that aren't based on truth.

The Conscious Mind

I like to think of the conscious mind as the human brain, because this is the part of our mind that makes us most human. This is the largest part of our brain from where we make all of our conscious choices. When talking about the human brain scientists often talk in terms of having the ability to hold 7 + or - 2 pieces of information.

What this means is that the human brain can hold between 5 and 9 pieces of information at any given moment. This is a really important concept for transforming our responses. When we respond from our human brain we normally make good choices and when we respond from our puppy brain we make emotional choices. Here is how this plays out:

Memory Study

Bristol University in the United Kingdom set up a study to explore the impact of this idea of 7 ± 2. They gathered students and told them that they were conducting a memory study. In classroom number 1 students were given a number between 3 and 10 digits long. They told the participants that the study was to test how they memorized information. The participants could memorize the number they were given however they liked. When they reported back the number they memorized they would also be asked to report the method they used to do so. The most useful methods of memorization would then be taught to students to help them in their studies.

This was not what the experiment was really about. The real experiment happened in the hallway.

After the participants were given the number to memorize they were asked to walk to the other end of the school to another classroom to report their number and memorization method.

As they walked down the hallway to the second classroom they came to a research assistant standing behind a table full of snacks. The research assistant would say, "Thank you very much for helping out with this important work. As a small thank you we have a treat for you but we only have enough treats for everyone to have one. You can either have a piece of fruit or you can have a cupcake."

What the researchers found was that if the participant was given a number that was 7 digits or larger they were much more likely to choose the cupcake. This does not mean that large numbers make us crave sugar, but instead it demonstrates that something as simple as a seven digit number is enough to fill our conscious mind and move us to a place where we will make a more emotional choice from our subconscious mind. Those who were trying to stick to a diet and eat healthily found it much harder to make a good choice because that 7 digit number was taking up the place where will power is. Because of this they reverted to the puppy brain to make an emotional choice, which this case was eating the cupcake.

The fact that something as simple as a 7 digit number makes it hard for us to make a good choice will be very important for us to understand as we move towards making better conscious choices and not just responding from our emotion.

Lessons We Can Learn From The Three Minds
There are two important lessons we can learn about how we respond in anger from this description of the three minds.

First, our subconscious mind is powerful. Some research has pointed to the fact that our subconscious mind is as much as 5000 times more powerful than our conscious mind. If the subconscious mind contains inaccurate information it will easily overwhelm the conscious mind, making us more likely to make emotional choices that we are likely to regret.

Second, it is easy to overwhelm our conscious mind. If we are hungry, angry, lonely, tired, or thinking about something else it is highly likely that we will make choices out of our subconscious mind, which again means we will make emotional choices that we are likely to regret.

Good News
But there is good news in all of this: we have the opportunity to change both of these things. We can transform the inaccurate information in our subconscious minds, like that a mouse is dangerous. We can do things that make sure our conscious mind isn't overwhelmed. By doing this we can ensure we make more conscious and fewer emotional choices, such as acting out of anger.

That is what all of the tools in the book do. Either they untangle inaccuracies on the subconscious level, and/or they clear the conscious mind of clutter.

Moving To The Now

As we explored in The Three Minds, our goal is to make good choices from the conscious mind. In that section I discussed Bristol University's study which tested the capacity of the conscious mind. The study showed that when the conscious mind is already filled with something, we are much more likely to make an emotional choice. The study found that people with more information to memorize were much more likely make a poor eating choice by choosing cake over fruit.

Memorizing numbers is not the only way that we can use up the capacity of our conscious minds. There are lots of thoughts, experiences, emotions, and physical states that can affect our ability to make good, conscious choices. We will look at this in chunks: the past, the future, and the current state. We will then look at what we can do to transform these states so that we are able to make good choices.

The Basics

In this section I will spend a lot of time talking about capacity. It is important that you understand what I mean by capacity. In this case I am talking about your capacity to make a good, unemotional choice. You know the difference between a thoughtful choice and an emotional choice. The more emotional we are, the more likely we are to make an irrational emotional choice.

For this example we will pretend that our mind has up to 10 units of energy to use in making good choices when we are faced with making a quick decision. (If it is useful, imagine a video game where your character is at full strength – ◉◉◉◉◉◉◉◉◉◉.)

To start with, it is the beginning of the day. You slept well, had a healthy breakfast, the drive into work was uneventful, and as you sit down at your desk you look at what you have planned for the day. You are ready for everything on the schedule. You are at full mental capacity of 10 – ◉◉◉◉◉◉◉◉◉◉.

As you are sitting at your desk a co-worker walks in to tell you that your 2pm meeting has to be re-scheduled for this morning and that you need to be in the conference room in 15 minutes. No big deal. You are sharp and focused. You gather everything you need for the meeting and head out the door.

The meeting goes well, but there has been a misunderstanding. The customer thought you were going to have more prepared than you did. They are annoyed and frustrated. They threaten to take their business elsewhere. You are able to talk them off the cliff, re-set expectations, and they leave satisfied.

You return to your desk happy it worked out, but you feel a little tired and unfocused because the meeting was more tense than it needed to be. Your mental capacity is still good, but not at full strength. You are at a 9 – ◉◉◉◉◉◉◉◉◉○.

After sitting at your desk for 15 minutes your computer starts to act up. You can't get any work done. You call technical support and they transfer you from one person to the next. Each time you have a new person on the phone you have to completely re-explain the problem. You are placed on hold for long periods of time. You are even disconnected once, making you start the whole process over. After 90 minutes your computer is working again.

You are frustrated at how much time you wasted, you are annoyed that the technical support people were incompetent, and now you are way behind on what you need to achieve for the day. Because of what has happened you have lost a lot of mental capacity. You are down to a 5 – ◉◉◉◉◉○○○○○.

The phone rings. It is your wife. She is going to be getting together with some of the girls this afternoon. She needs you to pick up the kids from school and take them to soccer practice. Because you're frustrated and at a 5 – ◉◉◉◉◉○○○○○ you snap at her.

You ask her why she couldn't have let you know this before you left this morning. You agree to pick the kids up and slam the phone down. You now need to figure out how you are going to get everything done at work and leave early to get the kids. You feel stressed. You are down to a 4 – ◉◉◉◉○○○○○○.

It's time your lunch. You are asked to join some of your co-workers to head to the all-you-can-eat pizza buffet for lunch. It is close and it will be quick with the food ready as soon as you walk in the door. You enjoy your co-workers and you laugh a lot during lunch. With the combination of the fun conversation at lunch, the energy surge of carbohydrates, and the walk to and from the restaurant on a nice sunny day you are feeling much better. You step back into the office with a new sense of purpose and energy. You are back up to a 7 – ◉◉◉◉◉◉◉○○○.

About 90 minutes after lunch you have a carbohydrate crash. All the sugars from the pizza have been digested and you feel like you are about to fall asleep at your desk. It is hard to focus on any one task. You skip from task to task, never seeming to get anything done. An hour passes and it feels like you have done nothing at all. In addition to being sluggish from lunch you are now frustrated that you are falling even further behind. You are now down to a 3 – ◉◉◉○○○○○○○.

It's now time to head home to get the kids. Traffic is a mess because of an accident and by the time you get to the school your kids are the only ones left because you are so late. The parent in charge of pick up is short with you because you are late. Your frustration grows. You are down to a 2 – ◉●○○○○○○○○.

The kids run into the house, grab their soccer stuff, then dash back out the car, you start driving to practice, to which you are already late, and then one of the kids announces that they only picked up one of their soccer cleats. Because you are at a 2 – ◉●○○○○○○○○ you lose it and start screaming at them.

This is not your normal response. It isn't that big of a deal. You are close to home so turning around will only add a few minutes to the drive. And really, it doesn't matter if your 7 year old is a few minutes late to soccer practice. But because your capacity was so low it was hard to make a good, conscious decision. Instead you made a purely emotional decision.

In the story above you can see how each moment of the day has the ability to affect our capacity to make conscious choices. Here are the things that affect our capacity in greater detail.

The Past

The first way we can lose capacity is by focusing our attention and emotions on the past. Whenever we feel guilty about an event that has already happened we send attention and energy towards something that we can't do anything about in the present moment. For example, you could have had a conversation with your spouse over breakfast where you were really annoyed with her. Because you hadn't completely woken up yet you said some things you regret. Now, as you sit at work you are still thinking about it. You want to go back and change what happened. You want to get hold of your spouse to let them know you are sorry, but you can't until they call you back.

By spending some, or a lot, of your attention on this incident that has already taken place, you have less capacity to focus on the present. Because of this you are much more likely to make an emotional choice right now.

The Future

In the same way that we can spend energy on regretting the past we can do the same thing by spending attention and energy on the future. Whenever we are worried about something coming up in the future, we are spending our capacity on something that isn't here. You know what it is like to be with someone who is worried about something in the future. It is as if they aren't present to us. They are almost in another place.

When we are worried, even if we are worried about what is coming in the very next moment, we spend our present capacity and are much more likely to make an emotional choice in the moment.

Our Present Physical/Emotional State

In addition to spending energy in the past and future there are lots of things that could happen in the present that will affect our capacity.

Anything that affects us physically will also affect our capacity. For example, if you are hungry or tired you will make more emotional choices. This is obvious. You know what it is like to try to do anything when you tired. The same is true of hunger. Whenever I travel with a certain friend I always take a few snacks because I know she quickly becomes crabby when she is hungry.

The same is also true when we are emotional. If we are angry, lonely, sad, feeling overwhelmed, or experiencing any other negative emotion, we will make more emotional decisions.

Finally, anything that affects our mental state will affect our capacity. Drugs and alcohol will obviously affect our ability to make good choices. We all know someone who becomes an angry drunk. It is important to note that this is true for all drugs, not just recreational drugs. It is possible that any drug, such as cold medicine or pain killers, could also affect your capacity.

What We Can Do

Once we recognize the way we interact emotionally with the past and future as well as what is happening in the moment, that affects our ability to make good conscious choices, we can do something about it.

You will notice that each of the tools in this book deal with one of these three areas. Every tool in this book is designed to help you to take advantage of your full capacity. The problem isn't knowing the right thing to do, it is being able to do it. When we act out of anger it's not because we think that it is the best choice. We do it because we don't have access to any other response. We don't have the capacity to make a good, conscious choice so we slip back into the emotional choice of anger.

By spending time working through these steps over and over again we continue to let go of the things we regret and things that are out of our control. By doing this we put ourselves in a place where we stop acting out of anger and start to make good choices.

It is important to note that just because we have the capacity to make a good choice doesn't mean that we will in fact make that good choice, but we are in a state that we are more likely to do so. We still have the ability to make any choice we want in the moment. By increasing our capacity we are more likely to make good choices for the short and long term, but there is no guarantee. We still need to be considerate, thoughtful people when we are making choices every day.

Stages Of Awareness

Now that we have looked at how the unconscious, subconscious, and conscious minds respond to situations we can explore the process of how we can move from making emotional choices out of anger to much more conscious choices.

After working with numerous clients, I've found that we move through 6 basic stages from feeling out of control and making extremely emotional choices, to being in control and being easily able to make conscious choices that bring us closer to our better selves.

For example, let's assume "Anne" is trying to deal with feelings that one of her co-workers has it in for her, undermining every choice she makes. As Anne does work with tapping on this issue she would move through these six steps.

Stage 1 Of Healing And Transformation: Unaware

In this stage we are completely unaware of the way our thoughts affect our emotions and how our emotions affect our choices. We are simply floating along, reacting to events. We don't feel like we have much control over what is happening in our lives.

It might look something like this:
- At work Anne completes a project.
- A co-worker comments, "I might have done it this way…"
- Anne feels like her co-worker is attacking her.
- She spends the rest of the day in a bad mood.
- In the future she continues to feel resentful towards her co-worker.

Stage 2 Of Healing And Transformation: Aware Well After The Fact

In the second stage we start to understand cause and effect, but it is well after the fact and it's only with a great deal of self-analysis. Generally in this stage someone must help us see the cause and effect.

It might look something like this:
- At work Anne completes a project.
- A co-worker comments, "I might have done it this way…"
- Anne feels like her co-worker is attacking her.
- Anne spends the rest of the day in a bad mood.
- After work Anne has a drink with a friend and she explains how her co-worker attacked her today.

- Anne's friend is able to help her see that maybe her co-worker was only trying to help her out by offering another option, not attacking her.
- Anne realizes that she overreacted.
- Once she sees what has happened she feels in a happier mood.

Stage 3 Of Healing And Transformation: Aware Right After The Fact

In the third stage you see how you are reacting to a situation. You still overreact, but shortly after the fact you understand what has happened.

It might look something like this:
- At work Anne completes a project.
- A co-worker comments, "I might have done it this way…"
- Anne feels like her co-worker is attacking her.
- Right after Anne gets mad she realizes her co-worker was just sharing her own experience. Anne might not agree with it, but she understands the spirit in which it was offered.

Stage 4 Of Healing And Transformation: Awareness As The Emotion Is Arising

In the fourth stage it feels like the world is starting to slow down a little. We recognize what's happening as the emotion arises. It is as if we are becoming a third party observer of our own experience. As it happens we will think, "This is what just happened, this is how I have interpreted it, and I am now reacting in this way." We may be quick enough to stop the emotional reaction.

It might look something like this:
- At work Anne completes a project.
- A co-worker comments, "I might have done it this way…"
- Anne very briefly feels like her co-worker is attacking her, but she realizes almost instantly that she's about to overreact. She hears her co-worker clearly.

Stage 5 Of Healing And Transformation: Awareness Of The Thought Which Leads To The Emotion

In the fifth stage it feels like the world has slowed down even more. In this stage we recognize the thought before the emotion. Once we recognize the thought, we can see how it is flawed. By recognizing that the thought is flawed we are able to stop the unwanted emotion before it has the chance to arise.

It might look something like this:

- At work Anne completes a project.
- A co-worker comments, "I might have done it this way…"
- Anne realizes three weeks ago if her co-worker had said this she would have felt like she was under attack.

Stage 6 Of Healing And Transformation: No Thought

Once you get to stage six, once again you don't notice anything happening, just as you didn't notice in stage one. But stage six is very different because the thought and emotional response occurring in stage one simply don't occur. In stage one you don't notice anything because you are unaware. In stage six you notice nothing because there is nothing to notice. You no longer feel like you are being attacked in any way, therefore there is nothing to react to.

It might look something like this:

- At work Anne completes a project.
- A co-worker comments, "I might have done it this way…"
- She thinks about their feedback.
- She might use it. She might not.
- Anne thanks him for his feedback and moves on with her day.

The Matrix

I think a great illustration of this is in the movie The Matrix. For those who didn't see the movie here is a quick recap of the critical points:

Neo, the main character played by Keanu Reeves, a brilliant computer hacker, is minding his own business living on the fringe. Through a series of events he is introduced to the idea that the world he perceives is not a real physical world. Instead what he is experiencing is a very realistic-feeling virtual reality experience. It's nothing more than a giant computer program that is giving him information. He is not simply watching a movie in his mind, but is actively interacting with the program. The program responds to his thoughts as actions.

Others who understand they are living in a virtual world persuade Neo to help bring down the system. As Neo learns more and more about the virtual reality system in which his mind is caught he also learns that he can control more than just his actions, he can also control other elements of the system because it's nothing more than information.

The most famous scene from the movie comes after Neo begins to assert control over elements in the system. One of three bad guys who had been sent to stop Neo fires a handgun at him. With his newly-gained control of the system Neo is able to slow the world enough to dodge the bullets.

At the beginning of the movie Neo is completely unaware of what is going on. Once he chooses to see that there is more at play than he had previously thought and that he might be able have some control, the world changes. At first he understands very little; he's more overwhelmed than before because he has little control. Because he is unable to process all he's been taught about the system, he feels like he has less control over his life than he had without this extra knowledge.

But as time passes he gains more knowledge and experience. He starts to understand how the world works and the things he can control. He sees more clearly what is illusion and what is real. As he does this he is able to see the world around him slowing down.

The scene where Neo is dodging bullets is the first time in the movie where he demonstrates a high level of control. This is very similar to stage 4 described above. He sees the trouble coming but is able to slow it down enough that he's not hit. In stage 4 we see the emotions arising from the thought, but since we are aware we stop them from affecting us and can choose not to act on them.

To extend this analogy even further:

Stage 1
- Analogy: We are shot but don't realize it. We let the wound fester, making us miserable.
- Real World: We feel we have no control over the world and no control over how we feel. Things happen and we suffer.

Stage 2
- Analogy: The bullet hits us, but we don't realize it right away. It is only after someone else points out that we have been hit that we seek medical attention.
- Real World: Something happens, making us feel like we are a victim of circumstances. We suffer emotionally until we understand what has happened. At this point we stop suffering. In this stage we do this because others help us to see what is happening

Stage 3
- Analogy: We are hit, but realize it right away. We seek immediate attention.
- Real World: Something happens, making us feel like we are a victim of circumstances. We suffer emotionally until we understand what has happened. At this point we stop suffering because are able to see what has happened on our own.

Stage 4
- Analogy: We see the bullet coming and get out of the way.
- Real World: As something is happening around us our emotions start to rise, but we recognize this right away and are able to deal with them quickly.

Stage 5
- Analogy: We recognize the gunman but get out of the way before a shot can be fired.
- Real World: We see what's happening and recognize how it might normally get an emotional charge out of us, but we remain in a state of peace.

Stage 6
- Analogy: The gunman never shows up.
- Real World: Situations that would have brought emotional charges in the past no longer mean anything to us, so we don't even notice the situations happening.

Depending on the severity of the issue, we will move through these 6 stages at different rates. In some cases we'll pass from stage 1 to stage 6 in just one round of tapping. In others, where issues have built up over years, like self-esteem issues, it will usually take much more time to move through the six stages.

Because you are holding this book you have recognized that you need to do some work on your anger. Either because someone has pointed it out to you (stage 2) or you recognize it yourself (stage 3). There might even be moments when you recognize your anger is getting the better of you and you make a new choice, like excusing yourself from the room (stage 4).

The primary reason it's important to understand these stages is that this helps us to understand how we are healing. A number of my clients have been frustrated that after doing so much work, they still haven't healed. They feel they haven't seen any improvement because they still have the same emotional responses. What they don't always realize is that they now recognize why they are overreacting, and they regain emotional stability much more quickly. Understanding these stages of healing enables us to see that we *are* healing.

What is interesting about these stages is how we can pass through them at different rates for different issues and different parts of our lives. We can be moving from stage to stage in one part of our life (for example, how we interpret what others say as judgment on us), while in another part of our life we are stuck in stage one, completely unaware of what is going on (such as why being around people in bad moods rubs off on us and brings us down).

For example, you might be in a situation where you get very angry at work, but are able to make a good choice about how you deal with that anger, but every time you get mad at your kids you lose it by yelling at them.

Remember the healing process is just that, a process. Some issues will take more time to heal than others. When we understand the process of this healing, we will identify this healing as it is happening, which will encourage us to continue working towards our goal.

Emotional Scale

Normally when we describe how we feel we do it in clear terms. We feel happy, sad, angry, frustrated, etc. In reality our emotions fall more on a spectrum than into hard and fast categories. Frustration and anger are different emotions but it is hard to tell where one feeling ends and the next one begins.

Here is one representation of an emotional scale from Esther Hicks' "Ask and It Is Given" (pg. 114):

1. Joy/Appreciation/Empowered/Freedom/Love
2. Passion
3. Enthusiasm/Eagerness/Happiness
4. Positive Expectation/Belief
5. Optimism
6. Hopefulness
7. Contentment
8. Boredom
9. Pessimism
10. Frustration/Irritation/Impatience
11. Feeling Overwhelmed
12. Disappointment
13. Doubt
14. Worry
15. Blame
16. Discouragement
17. Anger
18. Revenge
19. Hatred/Rage
20. Jealousy
21. Insecurity/Guilt/Unworthiness
22. Fear/Grief/Depression/Despair/Powerlessness

This is a far from perfect emotional scale, but it will be useful as a tool for our conversation.

You will notice that the most positive feeling emotion it at the top of scale at number 1 and the most negative feeling emotion is at number 22. Between emotion 7 contentment and 8 boredom is the dividing point between positive and negative emotions.

There a few key lessons that we can learn from looking at an emotional scale, but for this exercise I am going shorten the list for simplicity:

1.   Joy
3.   Happiness
5.   Optimism
6.   Hopefulness
7.   Contentment
8.   Boredom
9.   Pessimism
10.   Frustration
17.   Anger
19.   Rage
22.   Depression/Despair

Using It To Recognize Progress

There will be times when you are tapping for something and you will move up the emotional scale and it will not feel like progress because you are still feeling a negative emotion.

For example, you could have lost your job. It is something that happens out of the blue. You find out at the end of the day. You are stunned. You go home and go to bed because you don't know what else to do. You toss and turn all night. When the sun comes up in the morning you wake up and you feel completely depressed.

As you lay in bed somehow you get enough focus to decide to tap for the feeling of despair and depression. As you tap the feeling of depression starts to lift you start to get really pissed off. You are angry at your boss for firing you. You are angry your supervisor because he didn't warn you. You are angry at yourself for not seeing it coming.

The feeling of anger is no fun. Often we don't make good choices in anger, but anger is a step up the emotional scale from despair. When we feel despair everything is hopeless and we just lie in bed all day doing nothing. Anger is the emotion of fighting back. When we move from despair to anger we are moving from giving up to wanting to fight for ourselves.

You have just moved up the emotional scale. Even though the anger is not a fun emotion to feel you are closer to being no longer overwhelmed with emotion and you are closer to making better choices.

As you continue to lie in bed feeling angry you keep tapping. As you tap you start to take the edge off the anger. Now the anger has transformed into frustration. You don't have a job. It will be hard to pay your bills. It is a tough time to be looking for a job. You will have to dip into your savings to pay your bills. This is frustrating because you worked hard to save that money and it feels like a waste to use it now, but you are thankful it is there.

Again, in a vacuum being frustrated isn't the best feeling in the world, but you are no longer angry. When we act out of anger we are emotional and often over-react. Now that you are frustrated you are more likely to be thoughtful when you react to the situation. You still aren't completely emotionally clear. It is not pleasant to feel frustrated but it is much better than feeling angry.

You can see how it would continue as you moved up the emotional scale. As things started to feel better you would be pessimistic about the future and then eventually would move to hopeful as you recognize that this isn't the end of the world and you do still have opportunities.

The reason it is important to recognize this is so that we are able to see the progress we are making. It is easy to be caught up in the emotion we feel in the moment and not recognize that things are getting better. If you look at our example it would be easy to feel like the tapping isn't working because you have tapped and still feel extremely angry. It is no fun being angry, but it is so much better than the hopelessness of despair.

When we recognize the progress we are making it helps us to appreciate our efforts and encourages us to keep doing the work.

Emotionally You Will Move Close To Where You Already Are

The second important lesson that we can learn from the emotional scale is that typically we will not experience major swings of emotion. For example, if you are frustrated and something goes poorly then you are likely to slide into anger or if something goes well you might move to hopeful.

The exception would be if something major happens like the death of loved one, the loss of a job, or being given an unexpected promotion. In these cases it is possible to make a big jump in one direction or another, but for the most part this won't happen.

This means that we stay close to our current emotional state. If we are to avoid anger and frustration then we want our moment-to-moment emotional state to be higher up the scale. Doing daily work to keep ourselves in a healthy emotional state will help us to avoid moving into negative emotions such as anger.

How To Use The Emotional Scale

I don't expect you to memorize this emotional scale. By understanding the concept of the emotional scale it will help you to see more clearly what you are going through. When you exchange the feeling of depression for the feeling of anger it might not feel like you are making progress because both emotions are painful. When we understand the emotional scale we can see that progress is happening and it will help us to stay motivated to keep doing the work we need.

The People In Your Life Don't REALLY Want You To Change

The title of this section might feel a little harsh.

And it is harsh.

To be honest the title is written that way for shock value.

But even though there is some shock value to the title, there is a really important concept contained in it as well.

There are many people in your life who want better for you. They want you to heal. They want you to grow. They want so much better for you than you have right now. Many of them have already showed you support in lots of ways. They have encouraged you. They have done things for you. They have sat you down to have a hard discussion to tell you that you need to change.

This is wonderful. You are lucky to have people in your life who want better for you, but there is something to keep in mind:

Some people only want better for you as long as it doesn't require them to change.

As I have talked about a number of times in this book, we don't live in a vacuum. When we make changes it affects the people around us, whether they want it to or not.

Here are a few examples of how this plays out where your change affects other people in a negative way:

- You decide to get into shape. This includes working out and eating better. At first your family are happy you are making new lifestyle choices and are proud of you. But as time passes they start to feel guilty that they are not doing the same. They start to resent you because your choices are pointing out that they are doing a poor job of taking care of themselves. Because they are now feeling bad about themselves they start to treat you with resentment.
- You decide to go back to school to finish your degree. You parents are happy because they always wanted you to get a college degree. They know it will help you to find a better job. Since you are working full-time you start to take night classes. Between classes and studying you have much less free time. Because of this you have less time to spend with the family, which means you have less time to solve their problems. They start to feel like

you have abandoned them because their needs are not being met. Their lives are harder because you're not taking care of everything for them so they start to pick and at nag you.

I want to be clear. Not every change you make will impact the other people in your life and not every person in your life will resent the changes you are making. There will be people in your life who champion your change even though they also have to change because they want better for you.

I am also not saying that you shouldn't change because it is going make other people's lives difficult. I just want you to go into this with your eyes wide open.

You are not responsible for anyone else's happiness. You are allowed to change and grow. As a matter of fact, you should be striving to improve your life. As you make changes just know that there will be people in your life who will not want to change with you. Some of them will resist you in subtle ways and others will do so blatantly.

Keep after it. You know you want this change. The people in your life really want what is best for you, they are just human and worry about change, even when it only affects them indirectly.

Here is a tapping script to help you stay focused on change in the face of resistance from others. When you find yourself in a place where people are acting out towards you because you are making changes, all you need to do is read this script and tap to it. After you say each sentence out loud move to the next sentence.

I know that I need to change…I know I need to do things in a different way…When I make changes in my life…It will also change my relationships…And there are people who won't like this…Many of the people in my life want my life to be better…They want me to make better choices…They want me to have a better life…But they don't realize that when my life changes our relationship might change too…And when our relationship changes…They will not get the exact same thing they were getting before…Because our relationship is changing they will have to change as well…It is not my responsibility to keep everyone else happy…It is not my responsibility to help others maintain everything in the same way…When I change my relationships will change…And in the long term…This change will be a good thing…I give myself permission to make my life better and to change…Knowing full well not everyone will like it…They are not my responsibility… Changing my life for the better is my responsibility.

Making It Routine

You are not going to be able to change the way anger impacts your life by just reading one book. It is something that will take time and work. You will need to find a way to work regularly on these issues to make real change.

This is much like getting healthy. Working out once isn't enough. It is something that you need to make routine and work on regularly. As you know, making things routine isn't always the easiest of tasks. There can be lots of false starts.

It takes time to add new practices and habits to our lives. On average it takes between 14 and 21 days to establish a new habit because that is how long it takes to create the new neural paths in the brain associated with the new habit.

Until the habit is created when we are trying to do something new we are doing it simply on willpower. Willpower is very good at getting you out of the way of a speeding car. Willpower is very bad at creating new habits.

A big part of dealing with anger is making sure that we are in a better emotional state day to day. The less stressed and the healthier we are, the less likely we are to overreact in anger. Taking some time every day to tap, even if it is for just a few minutes, will go a long way to keeping you on an emotional even keel. Another benefit of tapping every day is by making tapping a regular habit, when something goes wrong and you are getting over emotional it will come to mind quickly as a way of dealing with whatever is going on.

Here a few tips that will make it much easier to make tapping (or anything else for that matter) part of your daily routine:

1) Start Small

To begin with you will be working on willpower alone. You know this doesn't work. You have tried adding things to your day, like working out, and you were successful for three or four days but then it fell away. Part of the problem was that you started too big. It is difficult to add something that will take 45 minutes a day. When starting something new it is best to start with something small.

When you are adding tapping to your daily routine it is best to start with just a little and slowly increase over time. I normally recommend that people add 5 minutes of tapping to the morning and 5 minutes of tapping before bed. You can get up 5 minutes earlier and adding 5 minutes to the end of the day isn't that big of a deal.

To start with just choose one tool or one tapping script from this book and take 5 minutes to tap. As time passes you can increase the time if you need it.

2) Attach Your New Habit To An Existing Habit

We are creatures of habit. So much so, some studies have concluded that 45% of all of our behaviors are habits. When in doubt our system will fall back into old patterns instead of adding something new. When adding something new it is much easier to tack the new habit on to a habit that already exists.

For example, I brush my teeth every morning and evening. When I decided to add tapping to my daily routine I decided to do it when I brushed my teeth. Regardless what the day looked like and regardless of what time I got up and went to bed, I always found time to brush my teeth. By choosing to tap at the same time I brushed my teeth I knew it was going happen most days.

You can choose anything that happens regularly. For example, my sister taps every day before she leaves work. On her way out the door she will step into the bathroom, lock herself in a stall so no one can see what she is up to, and will tap away any stress and worry from the work day so she doesn't go home with it.

It doesn't matter what you tie it to, but it will be easier to add a habit to something that is already happening regularly.

3) Do It In The Same Place

If you do something in the same place over and over again then that place will remind you of doing that task. I do all my prayer, relaxation exercises, and tapping seated in the same chair. When I look at the chair I can feel myself relax. I don't need to tap or even sit in the chair. I have trained my system to know that it is the place of relaxation.

By doing a new habit in the same place each time you will help to build the habit because everything about it is consistent.

Secondary Gain

Secondary gain is an important concept to understand when we are trying to make a change like getting our anger under control. It is a little subtle because it happens in a subconscious way.

Secondary gain is when there is a benefit to keeping situations or relationships the way they are, even when things aren't going as we would like. The easiest way to see this is through an example.

There is a widower. He wakes up early one morning and sees that it has snowed overnight. He decides that he needs to clear his walk. While shoveling in the dim morning light he stumbles, falls, and hurts his hip. Because of his injury his adult children are calling him every night to make sure he is OK, meals-on-wheels provide him with two meals a day, with the nice ladies who deliver the meal staying to chat a bit, and on Sunday afternoons the pastor from the church brings communion to the house.

On a conscious level the widower wants to heal. He doesn't like being in pain and he hates depending on other people to get things done. On a subconscious level it is a different story. Even if he is not willing to admit it, there is a part of him that really likes his children calling every night and he loves the company of all the visitors who are checking up on him.

The secondary gain in this case is all the positive attention that comes with the negative of his injury. When a situation like this happens there is a part of the system that will impede the healing process in the body because it knows that as soon as he gets well he will be lonely again.

There are actually two different types of secondary gain. The first is illustrated above, when there is a hidden benefit to a problem what we currently have. The other type of secondary gain is when something negative comes along with a positive. For example, I had a client who wanted to lose 35 lb but she said, "I have heard how all my friends, who are also overweight, talk about skinny people. They say the meanest things. If I lose weight then they will say those horrible things about me too."

It makes perfect sense that she would self sabotage her weight loss. Why would she do something that puts her at odds with her closest friends?

The problem with secondary gain is that it is powerful, can stand in the way of us achieving what we really want, and it can be hard to identify because it happens in a subconscious way. What is even more insidious is that the belief hindering our progress may not even be true. As in our second example, her friends might not really say mean things about her weight loss. They could even be encouraging and see her weight loss as a positive example and join her in making healthy eating choices. It doesn't matter if the belief is true or not, if it is present it will get in the way of the healing process.

Here are a few more examples of secondary gain:

- Wanting to quit smoking: If I quit smoking I won't have an excuse to leave my desk to take a break every two hours at work.
- Wanting to get rid of anger: My anger is keeping me safe because when I get angry I have the energy I need to fight back.
- Wanting to lose weight: If I lose the weight and then gain it back everyone will see that I am weak-willed.
- Wanting to do a really good job on a new project: If I succeed at this difficult project then everyone will expect me to be successful with all the difficult projects I attempt.

If you are having trouble changing something in your life more than likely there is an aspect of secondary gain that is standing in the way of transformation. In order to make the change you want it is important that you spend time working on secondary gain. Here are a few simple steps to work on this issue. I recommend that you return to this tool regularly as secondary gain can come up repeatedly during the healing process and, as you progress, it is possible that new types of secondary gain will show up.

Right now, to get a better understanding of secondary gain and how we start to transform it I would like you to work through these steps with anger. In the future you can use it for any part of your life that you are having a hard time changing.

1) Name The Issue You Want To Work On
Each issue will have its own secondary gain issues. It is best to work on one issue at a time. Name the issue where you want to see change.

> The change I want is…

2) What Is The Benefit Of Keeping The Issue At It Is?
Name the benefits that come with keeping the issue you want to change. It might take some time to come up with the list, but just think, "What is good about keeping things the way they are?" Come up with three benefits for your issue.

> The benefits of me keeping my issue the way it is are…
> And…
> And…

3) What Is The Downside To Making The Change You Want?

Change isn't always entirely positive. There are often negatives that come along with the positives. These could be adding more work, the opportunity to back slide, and/or changing other people's expectations. What are the negatives that could come with the change you want? Come up with 3 negatives.

> The downside to making this change is…
> And…
> And…

4) What Positive Benefits Will You Receive From The Change?

One of the fastest ways to defuse secondary gain concerns is to name everything you will achieve with the change. This includes the negative aspects you are letting go and the positives that you are adding. What negatives will you lose and what positives will you gain with this change?

> With this change I am going to get rid of…
> And…
> And..
> With this change I am going to gain…
> And…
> And…

5) Tap Through The Script

Take a nice deep breath and start tapping. Begin at the beginning of what you have just written. When you begin a new sentence move to the next tapping point. Tap through the script three times.

Once you have worked through these steps you will lessen the power of the secondary gain and you will be able to see when secondary gain is starting to slow your progress again.

Why Each Emotion Exists

One of the ways in which we can describe our body is by calling it an 'information system'. This means that the way it communicates what it needs and what it is experiencing is through information.

For example, when I place my hand on something hot it starts to hurt and the pain is my system saying, "Move! Your flesh is melting!" When my ankle hurts after a sprain my system is telling me I need to stop walking on my ankle so it can heal.

Our emotions are no different. They are information about how our system is understanding what is going on, with each emotion providing us with a specific piece of information. When we are able to understand this information it makes it easier for us to change and transform our experience.

Here is a list of emotions and what information they are conveying.

Anger

Anger conveys the information that a part of us feels like we are under attack. This does not mean that we are in actual physical danger in this moment and that someone is about to attack us. It simply means that there is a part of us that believes something or someone is coming after us.

For example, when I get angry at someone in a restaurant because they messed my order I know consciously that I am not being attacked. At the same time it is possible for part of me to believe the reason they are messing my order up is because they don't think I am very important, therefore they are dismissing me and my worth. If there is a part of our personality perceiving things in this way it will feel like an attack.

When we get angry we will be able to change our mood by asking ourselves the question, "Why might part of me feel under attack in this situation?" If we are able to ask this question we will see things more clearly and lessen the anger we are feeling.

Sadness

We feel sad whenever we feel we have lost or disconnected from something that is important to us. The most common experience of sadness is related to other people. We can feel sad when someone we love leaves us or dies. But we can also feel sad about missing out on other things that are important.

For example, I could lose what I thought was the perfect job. Not only am I losing out on the income from the job, but I am also losing the opportunity to do something I really enjoy. I am losing the experience and that is what the sadness is pointing out.

When we feel sad we can ask the question, "What thing, experience, or relationship do I feel like I am losing right now?" When we are able to answer this question we can see things more clearly. We will be able to appreciate the things we have had in the past and see what they mean to us. When this happens much of the emotional charge will come down.

Side note: As stated earlier, the goal of this book isn't to make you emotionless. The information that emotions bring us is important. When we lose someone we love it is perfect and appropriate that we feel sad. By asking questions about sadness we are not making it go away, instead we are trying to understand it so that we don't feel overwhelmed by it.

Frustration

We feel frustrated when things aren't going the way that we want them to. This is different from anger because when we feel angry we feel like something is after us. When we feel frustrated it is because our needs aren't being met.

For example, when I am on the phone with the cable company for 45 minutes, being transferred to another person every few minutes, and each time I having to re-explain my issue, I don't take this personally. I don't feel like they have it in for me, but I am not having my need of having my cable turned back on met in a timely fashion.

When we are frustrated we can ask the question, "What need, desire, or want to do I have that is not being met and why?" When we are able to do this we are able to slow our emotion and our emotional response.

The example of being stuck on the phone and being passed from person to person is something I find particularly frustrating. When I am able to ask myself this question and understand why I am so frustrated I can see what is going on and change what is happening.

When I notice I am getting frustrated and get transferred on more time on the phone I will say, "Right now I am really frustrated because I have been transferred four times and have had to explain everything over and over again. I am frustrated at the process. I am sorry if I get frustrated at you. I know it is not your fault, but I am just not having a good experience."

When I say something like this two things happens. First, I slow myself down because I am naming what is going and why. Second, I get much better service because I have been honest with what is going on in my head and the people I'm dealing with are now on my side because I am trying not to get frustrated with them.

Fear/Worry/Anxiety

Fear, worry, and anxiety are degrees of the same type of emotion so I have grouped them together. We feel these emotions when we are worried that something will go wrong in the future. This thing that could go wrong could be far into the future or it could be in the next moment, like what someone is going to say next.

When we feel fear or worry about something the question to ask ourselves is "What do I think could possibly go wrong?" When we ask this question it helps us to see things more clearly. When we ask the question about what we think might go wrong there are two possible outcomes.

First, we might name something that might really go wrong. For example, I might be worried I will ask Sally out on a date and she will turn me down. It is possible that she might say no, but when I look at it in these terms I am able to see what I can control and what I can't, which helps me to diminish the worry because I recognize that it is not the end of the world if she says no.

Second, we might see that what we are worried about isn't really a danger. I might be worried that if I give a presentation in front of a group it will go really badly, everyone will laugh about it, and I will be fired. When we name what the fear thinks will go wrong we are able to recognize that it is overreacting and be able to relax a little because we know the feared outcome isn't true.

Shame

When we feel shame it is because part of our system believes we have done something wrong. Often this feeling of shame is heightened by feeling that we should have known better before we made the bad choice. I am ashamed that I made the bad choice in the first place, and also because I knew it was going to be a bad choice before I made it.

The interesting part of shame is that we can feel it when in fact we have done nothing wrong. For example, it is very common for people who have been physically attacked to feel shame. The shame believes that they should have done things to protect themselves or that they should have known better to be in the place where they were attacked. Logically we can see that we are not responsible for the attack we received, but there is a part of us that doesn't believe that and therefore blames us.

When we feel shame we should ask ourselves the question, "What do I feel like I did wrong? Was it really wrong to do it? Am I taking blame for something someone else did?"

Because of the complexity of the emotion of shame, simply asking these questions isn't enough to release the feeling of shame, but is a good first step. If you are experiencing the feeling of shame I would encourage you to use the forgiveness tool in this book, but instead of offering the forgiveness to someone else, you will be extending it to yourself.

How To Use This Information

Now that we can see that emotions are a way for our body to let us know what we are experiencing there are two ways that we can use this information.

First, when we are able to give an emotion full voice it will be shorter lived. To give an emotion full voice I mean we are taking the time to listen very closely to the emotion and what it is about. We are moving from feeling fear to knowing exactly what we are afraid of. Often by simply going through this process the emotion will diminish because of our awareness of what the emotion is trying to communicate so that it doesn't need to be present any longer.

Second, we can use this information to tap on. By just acknowledging and understanding what an emotion is about won't always be enough to create a release. There will be times when as we ask the question to see what an emotion is about, we can in fact make the emotion stronger because we are now tuning into the details of the situation. Once we can see what is going on more clearly we put ourselves in a position to tap in a more efficient way around the issue.

In Part 5 of the book we will explore lots of tools that will help us to do just this. It is important to understand this concept so that you can respond to and understand more precisely what is going on when you feel an emotion.

Chapter 5 –
The Tools

Introduction

Now that we have spent time on understanding what anger is and how the healing process works we are going to jump into the tools you can use to start transforming the way you respond to anger.

The only way these tools will be helpful for you is if you spend time on doing them. Simply reading through the tools might give you a little more understanding of what is going on in your life, but it will not lead to any meaningful change.

The best way to use this part of the book is to set some time aside each day and only do one or two of these tools. As much as you would like to have your anger under control all at once, this will be a process that will take time. You will need to spend a little time every day doing this work.

The tools are organized in such a way that the simpler tools come first. This will help you to get a little better at tapping with each thing you try.

Please, please, please try each and every tool listed in this book. If there is a tool that feels uncomfortable to try and you really don't want to do it then make sure you do that tool. The tools that you find most uncomfortable are the most likely to correspond to an area of your life that really needs the work.

Remember, you are doing this work because you want to see a change in your life. This is not about working through the book to say that you have done a lot of things. The only way this will happen is if you honestly work through the steps of each tool.

Once you have worked through all the tools go back to the ones you liked, the ones that made the most difference, and the ones that were the hardest to do. Keep working through the tools over and over again.

If you do this, as we have seen many times before with the guys in my classes, it will make a real and lasting difference.

Negative Emotion: Formula One

One of the ways that we can do a better job of how we respond today is to take a look at the past moments where we responded in anger. With these past moments we are able to uncover what was going on in our thoughts. Once we reveal this we can tap for them so they do not show up in the same way in the future.

Here is a simple formula that you can use to tap for something that has happened in the past that you are still thinking about. Start by thinking of an event about which you still have negative emotions. The event can be something that was recent or it could be something that happened a long time ago.

When you think of something that happened it is possible that you will experience a number of emotions. For example, you might have had a fight with someone you love. As you think back to what happened you might feel betrayed because they brought up things from your past and you might also feel angry because they weren't listening to your side of the story.

When you use this with more than one emotion make sure you include all the information for each of the emotions.

1) Complete the following statements

A) Name a negative emotion(s):

B) Describe in detail what happened in a situation where you felt this emotion:

C) Describe in detail how it affected you when it happened:

D) Describe in detail how it is affecting you now:

E) Describe in detail all of the negative outcomes of this event when it happened:

F) Describe in detail all of the negative outcomes you are experiencing today from this situation:

G) Describe in detail how you feel about the outcomes:

H) Describe in detail all possible future negative outcomes from what happened:

I) Describe in detail how you feel about these possible future outcomes:

J) If you had the power to change anything about this situation describe in detail how you would change it:

2) Tap

Take your answers from above and insert them into the following script and tap through it. With each new sentence move to the next tapping point.

Even though I feel __(A)__ because __(B)__ happened, I love and accept myself.

I love and accept myself even though __(B)__ happened which made me feel __(A)__.

When I experienced __(B)__.

It affected me back then by __(C)__.

And it affects me today by __(D)__.

The negative outcomes of this were __(E)__.

And is __(F)__.

These outcomes make me feel __(G)__.

The possible future negative outcomes could be __(H)__.

These possible outcomes make me feel __(I)__.

I give myself permission to believe I can change this and have it become __(J)__.

Negative Emotion: Formula Two

In Formula One we looked at something that didn't work out in the past. Now we are going to look at something that isn't working out currently.

When something isn't working out the way we would like we know how we would like things to change, such as better relationships, more support, or more opportunities and there can be a lot of emotion that goes along with not having what we want.

We can feel frustrated that our needs or desires are not being met, overwhelmed that we don't know how to get to what we want, or angry because it just isn't fair how things are working out badly.

When this happens we spend a lot of emotional energy on the situation. This emotional drain makes it more difficult for us to make good choices in other areas of our lives, which in turn prevents us from working towards what we want.

Here is a simple formula that you can use to tap for something that you would like to see happen, whether is is something small or something big. What is important is that you are able to tune into the emotions you feel about what you want, and the emotions you feel about not having it.

When we do this type of tapping not only do we clear up emotions around the issue, we also make it easier to make better choices in the rest of our lives.

1) Complete the following statements
A) Name in detail what you would like to see happen:

B) Describe in detail how you will benefit by having this happen:

C) Describe in detail how others will benefit having this happen:

D) Describe in detail how you will feel when this happens:

E) Describe in detail how it feels right now not having this happen yet:

F) Write down three things you can do right now to move you closer to this happening:

2) Tap

Take your answers from above and insert them into the following script and tap through it. With each new sentence move to the next tapping point.

I would really like ____(A)____ to happen.

Even though ____(A)____ hasn't happened yet, I love and accept myself.

I love and accept myself even though ____(A)____ hasn't yet happened.

I want ____(A)____ to happen because it will give me ____(B)____.

I want ____(A)____ to happen because it will give others in my life ____(C)____.

When this finally happens I will feel ____(D)____.

Because it hasn't happened yet I feel ____(E)____.

Even though I don't have ____(A)____ yet, right now I can ____(F1)____, ____(F2)____, and ____(F3)____.

A_CD – What Is B?

One of the things that many of the guys in my classes have talked about is the fact that when they experience anger it feels like it just shows up out of nowhere. One moment they feel calm and the next they are in a fit of rage.

This is not how anger always happens, but when it does happen this way we are much more likely to make choices that we regret.

Even though it feels like the anger is coming out of nowhere there really is a thought that happens in a split second before we feel the anger. In this tool you are going to learn how to find that thought and how knowing that thought is a powerful tool to changing how much anger shows up.

Every situation seems to be made up of three parts:
- Stimulus: We see something happening or someone doing something.
- Response: We respond to it.
- Outcome: There is an outcome to our actions.

Here are a few simple reactions:
- The phone rings.
- We answer it.
- We have a conversation.

- A car is driving down the road.
- We move out of the way.
- We are safe.

- A friend is waving at us from across the room.
- We see them but return to our work.
- They feel frustrated because we didn't wave back.

In reality there is another step that happens so quickly that we don't even realize it. In the split second between the stimulus and the response there is a thought. Most of the time it happens so quickly that we don't realize it is there. Look at our three examples with the thought added.

- The phone rings.
- Thought: Someone is calling me.
- We answer it.
- We have a conversation.

- A car is driving down the road.
- Thought: I am in danger.
- We move out of the way.
- We are safe.

- A friend is waving at us from across the room.
- Thought: I really don't have time to deal with him right now!
- We see them but return to our work.
- They feel frustrated because we didn't wave back.

In the three examples above it is easy to recognize what the thought is between the stimulus and action but, as you will see, that is not always the case.

There is a specific reason for why it is important for us to figure out what the thought is between the stimulus and the action. When we spend time looking back at past events to figure out what the thought was, we literally rewire our brain by creating a new connection between the conscious mind and the unconscious mind. The more often we do this the stronger this new path between the conscious and unconscious mind will become.

The new path we create is very useful because it slows down our responses. Those thoughts that happen so quickly that we aren't conscious of them taking place now happen in such a way that we are aware that we have a choice so that our emotional response is no longer unconscious.

In many cases this might not feel like that big of a deal. When the phone rings, it doesn't matter whether or not I give it much thought before I answer it. But when it comes to emotional responses this is extremely significant.

This is what we talked about at the beginning. One moment we are fine and the next moment we are throwing punches.

This might not mean making best choice right away, but when it comes to emotional responses a split second can make all the difference. For example, something makes me really mad and I can feel my rage growing. Because I have spent time working on what the thoughts are before my actions, I am able to have that split second to understand what is really going on. As the anger grows inside me and I feel like I need to hit the person in front of me I can see that that is a very bad choice and I am able to redirect my anger and hit the wall instead.

Hitting the wall isn't a good choice. It is painful. It could cause permanent damage. It could destroy part of the wall. BUT when I hit a wall I won't be arrested for assault.

So while hitting the wall isn't a great choice, it is so much better than hitting a person.

When we slow down our responses by a split second we move from:
- Saying something really stupid and mean to just hanging up the phone.
- Tailgating the guy who just cut us off to just screaming a few curse words.
- Assuming the reason my friends showed up late is because they don't think I am worth a phone call to recognizing that there are lots of reasons they might be late.

That split second becomes a powerful tool. When we are able to move away from a purely emotional reaction will make a huge difference in the responses we make.

A_C what is B?
Using this to create the new paths in our brain is straightforward.

1) Choose an emotion you would like to work on
I have found it most useful to work on a number of past events for one specific emotion. This will help us to identify patterns in our behavior. You can come back to do the process as many times as you like for as many emotions as you like.

Common emotions to use in this process:
- Anger
- Sadness
- Frustration
- Jealousy

2) Come up with a list of instances when you felt the emotion
For this example we going to use anger. You list might look like this:
- A: My boss didn't return my call.
- B:
- C:

- A: My sister took my car without asking.
- B:
- C:

- A: The dog puked in the living room last night and my roommate who was home did nothing about it.
- B:
- C:

- A: My girlfriend called me lazy.
- B:
- C:

3) Add your response to each moment:

- A: My boss didn't return my call.
- B:
- C: I sent him a nasty email telling him how mad I was.

- A: My sister took my car without asking.
- B:
- C: I called her and cussed her out.

- A: The dog puked in the living room last night and my roommate who was home did nothing about it.
- B:
- C: I scooped up the puke and put it in my roommate's bed.

- A: My girlfriend called me lazy.
- B:
- C: I threw the TV remote control at her.

4) Add the thought that took place between A and C:

This is the step that will take the most time and thought. In some cases it will not be immediately obvious what the thought was before you made your response. You are trying to figure out the logic behind the emotion, which can be hard but the more you do this, the better you will become at it.

- A: My boss didn't return my call.
- B: He doesn't care about me or value the work I do.
- C: I sent him a nasty email telling him how mad I was.

- A: My sister took my car without asking.
- B: My sister thinks I am only here to meet her needs.
- C: I called her and cussed her out.

- A: The dog puked in the living room last night and my roommate who was home did nothing about it.
- B: My roommate is the laziest person I know and he thinks I am his personal maid.
- C: I scooped up the puke and put it in my roommate's bed.

- A: My girlfriend called me lazy.
- B: My girlfriend thinks the world revolves around her and my job as a boyfriend is to serve her when she snaps her fingers.
- C: I threw the TV remote control at her.

Important note: Sometimes people have trouble doing this process because after the fact we are able to see clearly that the thoughts we had in the moment aren't true. For example, there is a part of me that is responding emotionally to fact that my boss didn't call me back. My emotions might think that he isn't calling me back because because he doesn't like me but in reality his mobile phone battery might be dead or he has switched it off while he is in a meeting.

Now that you have an idea of what we are talking about I want you to work through the steps above with the emotion of anger. Think of five times recently when you experienced anger and work them all the way to the end.

Side Note On Outcome AKA What Happened To D?

When we started there were four parts to each moment: Stimulus, Thought, Response, and Outcome. You will notice that in the exercise above I didn't spend any time talking about the outcome of our choices. The outcomes of our choices are important, but we need to be careful when using the outcomes as the main factor we look at to see if we made a good choice. There are times where we can make the best choice and get a bad outcome and other times when we can make the worst possible choice and get a great outcome.

One of the guys from my class served as a perfect example of this. His pattern was to go out with his boys on Friday nights after work, drink too much, and end up in a fight. This would happen for a number weekends in a row. Because he was so big he normally didn't get hurt too badly. One weekend everything changed because there happened to be a group of off-duty police officers in the bar when he started his usual fight. He was arrested for second degree assault.

Up until his arrest he didn't think his drinking and fighting were a big deal because the outcome had always been fine.

Just because we are getting the outcomes we desire it doesn't mean that we are making the best choices. As you look back at past events it is good to learn from the outcomes of our choices, but it shouldn't be the only thing we look at when trying to measure success.

Emotion List

In tools that you have tried up to this point I have stressed that when answering questions about your thoughts and emotions you need to be as specific as possible. The more specific we are when describing an issue, the faster we will find relief. Sometimes we think we are being specific when we really aren't being as specific as we could be.

When we are working on one of the tools in class and I ask the guys how they are feeling at any given point I am usually given a one word answer. "Angry." "Sad." "Confused." I normally ask a follow-up question along the lines of "[insert emotion] how?"

The reason I do this is because there are many different shades to emotions. There is "angry = I need space" and "angry = I want to punch the wall." The more specific we are with the particular shade of the emotion, the easier it will be to clear it out.

Below you will find a list of negative emotions, positive emotions, and physical and emotional needs created by The Center For Nonviolent Communication. The list is helpful when you are trying to describe your emotions.

When you are working with any of the tools in this book the list can be very useful. Here are three ways that you can use this list right now based on the work we have done so far. Before moving to the next tool in the book try all three of these.

- Take one of the emotions from the negative emotion list below and use it with Formula One.
- Take one of the emotions from the positive emotion list below that you would like to have more of in your life and use it with Formula Two.
- Take one of the needs from the physical and emotional needs list below that you would like to have more of in your life and use it with Formula Two.

Negative Emotions

AFRAID	AVERSION	DISQUIET
apprehensive	animosity	agitated
dread	appalled	alarmed
foreboding	contempt	discombobulated
frightened	disgusted	disconcerted
mistrustful	dislike	disturbed
panicked	hate	perturbed
petrified	horrified	rattled
scared	hostile	restless
suspicious	repulsed	shocked
terrified		startled
wary	**CONFUSED**	surprised
worried	ambivalent	troubled
	baffled	turbulent
ANNOYED	bewildered	turmoil
aggravated	dazed	uncomfortable
dismayed	hesitant	uneasy
disgruntled	lost	unnerved
displeased	mystified	unsettled
exasperated	perplexed	upset
frustrated	puzzled	
impatient	torn	**EMBARRASSED**
irritated		ashamed
irked	**DISCONNECTED**	chagrined
	alienated	flustered
ANGRY	aloof	guilty
enraged	apathetic	mortified
furious	bored	self-conscious
incensed	cold	
indignant	detached	
irate	distant	
livid	distracted	
outraged	indifferent	
resentful	numb	
	removed	
	uninterested	
	withdrawn	

FATIGUE
beat
burnt out
depleted
exhausted
lethargic
listless
sleepy
tired
weary
worn out

PAIN
agony
anguished
bereaved
devastated
grief
heartbroken
hurt
lonely
miserable
regretful
remorseful

SAD
depressed
dejected
despair
despondent
disappointed
discouraged
disheartened
forlorn
gloomy
heavy hearted
hopeless

TENSE
anxious
cranky
distressed
distraught
edgy
fidgety
frazzled
irritable
jittery
nervous
overwhelmed
restless
stressed out

VULNERABLE
fragile
guarded
helpless
insecure
leery
reserved
sensitive
shaky

YEARNING
envious
jealous
longing
nostalgic
pining
wistful

Positive Emotions

AFFECTIONATE	EXCITED	EXHILARATED
compassionate	amazed	blissful
friendly	animated	ecstatic
loving	ardent	elated
open hearted	aroused	enthralled
sympathetic	astonished	exuberant
tender	dazzled	radiant
warm	eager	rapturous
	energetic	thrilled
ENGAGED	enthusiastic	
absorbed	giddy	**PEACEFUL**
alert	invigorated	calm
curious	lively	clear headed
engrossed	passionate	comfortable
enchanted	surprised	centered
entranced	vibrant	content
fascinated		equanimous
interested	**GRATEFUL**	fulfilled
intrigued	appreciative	mellow
involved	moved	quiet
spellbound	thankful	relaxed
stimulated	touched	relieved
		satisfied
HOPEFUL	**INSPIRED**	serene
expectant	amazed	still
encouraged	awed	tranquil
optimistic	wonder	trusting
CONFIDENT	**JOYFUL**	**REFRESHED**
empowered	amused	enlivened
open	delighted	rejuvenated
proud	glad	renewed
safe	happy	rested
secure	jubilant	restored
	pleased	revived
	tickled	

Physical and Emotional Needs

CONNECTION	PHYSICAL WELL-BEING	AUTONOMY
acceptance	air	choice
affection	food	freedom
appreciation	movement/exercise	independence
belonging	rest/sleep	space
cooperation	sexual expression	spontaneity
communication	safety	
closeness	shelter	**MEANING**
community	touch	awareness
companionship	water	celebration of life
compassion		challenge
consideration	**HONESTY**	clarity
consistency	authenticity	competence
empathy	integrity	consciousness
inclusion	presence	contribution
intimacy		creativity
love	**PLAY**	discovery
mutuality	joy	efficacy
nurturing	humor	effectiveness
respect/self-respect		growth
safety	**PEACE**	hope
security	beauty	learning
stability	communion	mourning
support	ease	participation
to know and be known	equality	purpose
to see and be seen	harmony	self-expression
to understand and be	inspiration	stimulation
understood	order	to matter
trust		understanding
warmth		

(c) 2005 by Center for Nonviolent Communication
Website: www.cnvc.org
Email: cnvc@cnvc.org
Phone: +1.505-244-4041

About, To, As If

One of the areas that causes us the most anger is our relationships. We get angry when people don't live up to their word, when they lie, and when they put us down.

One of the questions I am asked most often is, "Can I tap to change someone else's behavior?"

The truth is we can't change someone else's choices, but there are two things that we can change in a relationship. We can change our own emotional response and we can change the space we create for someone else which allows them to make new choices.

When we change these two parts of a relationship it will put us in a place where we are much less likely to get angry.

Of all of the tools I teach, this is by far my favorite and one of the most powerful. Please take the time to learn this tool. It is very straightforward and as you will see it is also flexible and can be used in many situations.

Our Response

You have an emotional response to every person in your life. When you think of some people it makes you feel happy and when you think of others you can instantly feel the stress building in your body.

These emotions we feel affect the way we approach people. I will be open to a request from someone I trust yet I will hesitate even to answer the phone when someone who drives me nuts calls.

These negative reactions aren't pleasant, they color our interactions, and they can even cause us to overreact.

A perfect example of this is a conversation between a mother and her teenage daughter. The daughter is heading out the door for the evening. As she reaches the door her mother asks, "What time are you going to be home tonight?" The daughter turns back and screams, "Why don't you trust me?" and storms out of the house.

The daughter has assumed that her mother doesn't trust her. Because this is her assumption, anything her mother asks will go through that emotional filter. It is likely that the mother was just trying to plan her evening, but the daughter immediately turned it into a major issue.

When we are able to take the emotional edge off our relationships we are able to see things much more clearly, making us less likely to overreact. When we don't overreact we prevent situations from escalating.

I am not saying that we should become other people's punch bags. I am not saying that we shouldn't stand up for ourselves and our needs. But if we start from a place that is calmer emotionally we will make better choices about the interaction, making it easier for everyone involved.

The Space For The Relationship

Every relationship we have is a co-creation between ourselves and the other person. They bring half and we bring half. If we change our half of the relationship then we change the nature of the relationship.

For example, there is someone at work who picks on you all the time. Every time they see you they make fun of how you dress, how messy your desk is, or how little you earn. You don't like it, but you don't stand up for yourself. There is a reason the other person is bullying you. More than likely they aren't happy with what is going on in their own life so to make themselves feel better they decide to put you down.

At a certain point you decide that enough is enough. You don't make a big scene, but you pull your co-worker aside and tell them that you don't appreciate being made fun of and if it continues you will stand up for yourself in front of everyone else. You have changed your side of the relationship by deciding you will not put up with being bullied. Since you are no longer allowing the your co-worker to put you down and providing him with an ego boost, he will probably stop picking on you and find a new way to boost his fragile ego.

You changed your side of the relationship and so the nature of the entire relationship had to change.

This can also be true for good relationships. We can change the way we are which allows the other person space to make different choices. I spend a lot time speaking to and working with youth groups. Time and again I will hear children say, "I love youth group. It is the only place that I can be myself. At school everyone fits into cliques. At home my family is crazy. Here I can be myself."

What the kids are saying, without knowing it, is that the leaders of the group have created a safe, loving space where kids know that they can be who they really are without judgement or ridicule. The leaders have changed their side of the relationship which has created space. They are not forcing the kids to act differently, but because they have created and are holding this loving space it allows the kids to make new choices.

What Happens When We Tap In This Way

The Process

The process itself is straightforward. Initially you will tap for only one relationship. You can use this for all types of relationships, but we need to work on them one at a time.

Choose one relationship you would like to tap for. While doing this process all you need to do is tap from one point to the next and follow these three steps. While you are doing these three steps you will tap the whole time. Just move from tapping point to tapping point to tapping point. Tap six to eight times on each point. Once you get started your hand will very easily move from point to point with little effort.

1) Talk About

In the first step all you need to do is describe the nature of the relationship. Simply imagine that you are sitting down with a friend you haven't seen in a long time and you are catching them up with what is going on in your life. The two key points are to describe the situation in as much detail as possible AND to share how each of these details make you feel. For example:

> *I am having a really hard time with my mother. Nothing I do is good enough for her. I stop by her place every night after work. I clean up her kitchen. I pay her bills. I cook her dinner. The entire time I am there she goes on and on about how great my brother is. How he does this so well and how he does that so well. But he never comes by to help. He calls my mother once a week and she thinks he is the greatest thing in the world. I am really hurt that my mother doesn't appreciate all the work I am doing for her. I feel a little jealous that my brother is getting all the praise. I feel like I am wasting my time because my mother doesn't even say thank you. I feel bad because my mother has had a really hard life and I should be grateful for all she has done for me. I feel bad for resenting her because of how much harder she had it than me.*

You can see it is very simple. You are "Talking About" what is going on and how it feels. With each detail we share the emotions we feel. Some of the details will have a number of emotions (it makes me sad, angry, and hurt). The more detail we come up with about the relationship and the more detail we come with about the emotions we are feeling, the more effective this tool will be.

2) Talk To

In the second part of this process we will imagine that we have the chance to talk to the person we are having a problem with and they are going to hear us clearly and understand everything we are sharing. It is important to note we are still doing this process alone. We are not seeking this person out. Often the people we have trouble with would not be able to hear or be open to what we are sharing. This is a process that we are doing for ourselves. We just need to imagine we are having this conversation.

As you continue to tap, go through everything you would want to share with the person. Share the things you are unhappy about. Share the things that hurt you. Share the things you wish they would hear. Share the things you wish they knew about themselves.

On the surface this might look like you are just going to be complaining and it might not feel very good to think these thoughts. There are two things to keep in mind. One, yes, it is true most of the things you will share are the things that are hard for you, but it is important to be honest with what you are feeling in order to heal this. Two, you also have the chance to share the things you hope for them. For example, the relationship that you are tapping for might be with someone who has an drug problem. In addition to sharing how much you are being hurt by their choices you can also share what you would like to see better for them. You might want to share with them "that they are better than this…that you don't want them to suffer…that you want them to find the things they love come back into their life…that you want better for their health."

This step is just an opportunity to say everything you would want to tell them. It might look something like this:

> I want you to know the choices you are making are really hurting me. I hate the fact that you never say anything nice about all the work I do for you. It really makes me feel jealous when you go on and on about my brother. He doesn't do anything for you and yet you only say nice things about him. You never say anything nice to me about what I do for you. I don't need you to praise everything I do. You don't have to stop talking about my brother. I just want you to realize that it would be nice to know that you notice me. I love you very much. I know you have had a hard life. I want to be there for you. I want to be helpful. I want you to know I love you. But the way you treat me makes it very hard to want to come back and help. I want to helpful. I want you to know I love you. But I need you to treat me better whilst I am doing it.

This is a straightforward step. You are pretending that you are "Talking To" the other person. There is nothing holding you back. You are in a safe space where you don't need to worry about how they will react. Say everything you want them to know and hear.

3) As If
The third step of the process is a little different. In the first two steps you were speaking from your point of view and your emotions. This is something that is easy to do because it is what we know

best, ourselves. In this step we will need to guess a little bit. We are going to imagine the relationship from the other person's point of view.

To do this step you need to pretend you can read the other person's mind and intentions. You are going to describe from their point of view why they are acting as they do.

It is important to note that when we try to understand why someone is acting the way they are we are not saying that we agree with the choices they are making, we are not saying we like those choices, and we are not saying that we want them to keep acting this way. We are just trying to understand it from their point of view. It might look something like this:

> *I know my mother is very lonely and the fact that my brother never calls her probably hurts her feelings a lot. If she were to admit that he is too involved in his own life it would really hurt her feelings. By going on and on about how great he is and successful he is in business my mother doesn't have to face the fact that he is too busy to spend time with her. I have a feeling the reason my mother gives me such a hard time, even when I am showing up to help, is because she has never known how to say nice things about people. She might be afraid that if she says nice things to me I will let up and not work so hard. Her whole life she has used scolding and put downs as a way to get us to do more. She might think she has to keep putting my work down to motivate me to do more. I know she is lonely and I am sure she is scared. She just doesn't know how to relate to me and she reaches for what is easy. Picking on me.*

Now it is quite possible that we could be completely wrong about why the other person is making the choices they are making, but by trying to understand it from their point of view it will soften our emotions. This does not mean that we should let them continue to run us over or treat us poorly, but when we see why they are acting the way they are it makes it easy for us to respond calmly and gracefully.

Very Flexible

This technique is very flexible and it can be used for many types of relationship.

You don't need to do each part for the same length of time. Recently while working with a client we spent close to 45 minutes on just step one, but only spent a total of 15 minutes for steps two and three. You might be very clear on how you feel about something and only spend two minutes on the first step, but you might have a backlog of things you would like them to hear that have been building up for years and you need to spend a lot of time with step two.

You don't need to do it in this order. I have found in most cases it is easiest to do it in this order, but if you want to start with step two because you have a clear sense what they need to hear, then start with step two.

You don't even need to do each part each time you tap. Some relationships are so big that one tapping session will not be enough. That is OK. When you come back to tap you can do part one and part two. Another time you might do part one and part three. Or because of time you might be able to work just on part one and nothing more.

You can use this technique for any relationship. You can use this technique for someone you see every day. You can use it for someone you will never see again, such as a family member who has died or someone who lives in another part of the world. You can even do this process for someone you have never met, such as someone who hurt one of your loved ones but who you will never meet.

What is most important is that you spend time with each part. Each part helps you to heal and clear your emotions in a specific way and they are designed to work together. By doing this you will make sure that you are emotionally clear when you approach others, which will make it easier for you to make good choices that are not overly emotional. Also, by doing this you will create space for others in your life to make better choices.

Action Step

1) Choose a relationship you would like to tap for.

2) What are the emotions you feel when you tune into this relationship?

3) Tap through the three steps described above.

4) Answer these questions
> What are the feelings you now have about the relationship?
> What did you learn about the other person while you tapped?
> What did you learn about yourself while you tapped?

Pre-emptive Tapping/People Who Push Our Buttons

No matter how much control we have over life there will be situations we encounter and interactions with people that we don't like. Even though we don't have control over these situations we can control our attitude and in turn control how we respond. If we go into a situation with a bad attitude then it is more than likely that we will have a negative experience. But if we go into a situation with our eyes open to what might go wrong then we have the opportunity to make better choices. This is particularly true for interactions with those people who push our buttons.

For example, there is someone in your life who is insecure about their own life and who they are. The way they compensate for this is to put down those around them. Because they have used this tactic for most of their life they very good at it. Subconsciously they are able to assess the person in front of them and know exactly how to cut that person down by commenting on their work, their love life, or the choices their children are making.

When we come across someone like this it can feel very personal and hurtful when they go after us because they are pointing out something that feels true. But if we are able to walk into this situation with the insight that they will try to push our buttons to feel better about themselves we can be in control of our interaction. When they start to come after us we are able to recognize that they don't really believe what they are saying, but are just trying to make us feel bad so they can feel better about themselves. In seeing through their tactic it becomes easier for us not to take their words so personally and move on without becoming emotionally involved.

If we are able to name the people and situations that cause an emotional reaction before we encounter them then we will be able see them for what they are and make better choices in how we react.

For example:
- I know the lines will be long at the DMV and so I am going to accept that and not feel rushed or stressed that I have to wait to be served.
- I know my mother will make a comment about how she wishes I would get married and instead of getting upset or defensive I am just going to change the subject.
- I know there will be lots of traffic at 8am on my way to work and I am just going to make sure I have some good music to listen to and enjoy the time alone with my thoughts.

If we take a little time to tap through these situations before they happen then we will react to them better now and in the future.

Action steps

1) Describe in detail a situation or person who pushes your buttons

Describe what they do or what happens, how it makes you feel (list all the emotions), and in what way you react to this that you don't like. To do this complete the following in as much detail as possible:

- This is what normally happens…
- It makes me feel…
- When I feel this way I normally respond by…

2) Describe in detail why things happen this way

If it is a situation it might be something like, "The DMV is a broken system, with underpaid and overworked people." For a person it might be, "They always pick on me because they need to make themselves feel better." In many cases when you describe the actions of another person you will be guessing as to why they are doing what they are doing. Complete the following in as much detail as possible:

- The reason it happens this way is because…

3) Describe in detail how you would like to see things differently

When you do this describe how you would like things to work differently, how you would like others to act differently, how you would like to respond differently emotionally, and how you would like to act differently. As each situation is unique you may not have answers to all of these questions, but answer all that apply in as much detail as possible.

- Instead of how it has happened in the past I would like the situation to play out like this…
- Instead of how others have acted in the past I would like them to …
- I would like to respond emotionally like…
- When this happens I would like to react by…

4) Describe in detail how you would like to see things happen differently

There are many things in our lives that we can't change, but in naming the other possibilities and possible outcomes we are more open to them happening. Complete the following with as much detail as possible (come up with at least three):

- I know that I don't control everything and there are some things that won't change, but the way I would like this to work out is…

5) Describe in detail the choices you can make right now to make the situation or relationship easier and better

When we see things more clearly for what they are and why they happen, we are able to see the new choices available to us. This does not mean that we are giving in or letting people take advantage of us but there are things we can do to make the people and situations in our lives more bearable by the choices we make. In as much detail as possible complete the following (come up with at least three):

- I know that I can't do everything differently but the things I can do differently to make this situation easier are…

6) Tap through the work

Take everything you have written above, read it aloud, and tap along to each of the phrases. Move to a new tapping point with each new phrase.

7) Reflect

Now that you have tapped through everything you have written how does the situation feel different and how do you feel different? Complete the following:

- I understand this about the situation…
- I understand this about myself…

What Is Forgiveness?

One of the many things that can affect us if we respond with anger is what we bring to this moment from the past. If we are holding a grudge or hard feelings towards someone then we will much more likely to react by exploding in a fit of anger.

In order to move on and prevent these past moments impacting our present, we need to be able to forgive others, BUT one of the most difficult parts of any healing process is forgiving others and forgiving ourselves.

When we forgive someone else it can feel like we are saying what they did was OK, it is OK for them to do it again, that we wanted it to happen, or that we would want it to happen again.

That is not what we are doing!

In reality when we forgive someone else what we are really doing is freeing ourselves. I know that might not make sense at first glance, but let me explain…

More than likely most of the people you are mad at and are holding a grudge against aren't thinking about you at all. They have hurt you or taken advantage of you and they have moved on.

You might think about how they hurt you every day or even multiple times a day. You are letting what happened consume your thoughts and energy, while on the other hand they are just going about their life, happy as can be.

When we hold a grudge against someone it is like we are wishing bad things on them but we are the ones taking the poison.

When we forgive someone else we are not doing it for them. We are doing it for ourselves. I want to be very clear about what forgiveness is and what it is not.

Forgiveness is NOT:
- saying that we like what happened
- saying we are happy it happened
- saying that they can do it again
- saying they shouldn't be punished for what they have done
- saying that someone else can do it to us
- saying that we deserved what happened
- saying we caused it to happen

- saying they can do it to someone else
- saying we are going to forget what happened
- saying we are going to miss the lesson in what happened

Forgiveness is choosing no longer to be an emotional prisoner to our past.

When I forgive, this is what I am saying:

> *What happened in the past sucked! I hate the fact it happened! I hate the fact that someone hurt me or took advantage of me. They have to take responsibility for their action. They have to deal with the consequences. I am going to learn from what happened. I am going to do everything I can to make sure it doesn't happen again. As I let it go I am choosing no longer to be stuck in this past event. As I let go I am not going to spend any more energy on this past event. I am forgiving not for their sake, but for my own. Forgiveness is all about me. I no longer need to be stuck in this.*

That is what happens when we forgive.

Here is a straightforward process to help you work through forgiveness in a way that ensures your needs are met and that you are no longer stuck in the past.

1) Answer the following questions describing who you have not forgiven and what they did to you that you can't forgive

A) Name someone who has hurt you that you haven't forgiven. If there are multiple people who hurt you at the same time and in the same way, do this process once for each of them. Even though they did the same thing to you, different people affect you in different ways. For example, your brother and father might have done the exact same thing to you, but you would have a different emotional response to the event because a relationship between brothers is different from a father-son relationship.

   The person who hurt me is…

B) Describe in detail what they did to you and include as many details as possible.

   What they did to me was…

C) Describe how you were affected at the time of the action. How were you hurt? What did you lose? What feels like it can never be changed?

   When it happened it affected me by…

D) Describe how it is still affecting you. Even though this is something that happened in the past it's possible you are still experiencing the consequences today. How does it affect the opportunities you have now, the choices you make, how you see yourself, and how you see others?

Even though it happened in the past it is still affecting me by...

2) Tap through the answers you have written above

Take a deep breath and start tapping. Read everything you have written above aloud. When you reach a new sentence move to the next tapping point. If new information comes to mind as you are tapping, stop tapping and add the new information before continuing.

3) Tap through the following script

If I choose to forgive (insert name); I am NOT saying that I like what happened.

If I choose to forgive (insert name); I am NOT saying I am happy it happened.

If I choose to forgive (insert name); I am NOT saying that they can do it again.

If I choose to forgive (insert name); I am NOT saying they shouldn't be punished.

If I choose to forgive (insert name); I am NOT saying that someone else can do it to me.

If I choose to forgive (insert name); I am NOT saying that I deserved what happened.

If I choose to forgive (insert name); I am NOT saying I caused it to happen.

If I choose to forgive (insert name); I am NOT saying they can do it to someone else.

If I choose to forgive (insert name); I am not doing it for them. I am doing it for me.

If I choose to forgive (insert name); I am choosing no longer to be emotionally tied to what happened.

More than likely they have forgotten about the incident. As I keep reliving it in my mind I am keeping myself prisoner to the moment. They are not keeping me there. I am.

If I choose to forgive I am not giving them anything. I am giving myself freedom to leave the moment.

Forgiveness is for me. It is not for them. I don't need to do anything for them. But I am worthy of forgiveness for me.

Repeat this tapping scrip 2 times.

Tapping To Give Thanks

In Part 4 we talked about the emotional scale. The higher we are on the emotional scale the harder it is for us to end up in a negative emotion like anger. By using gratitude and thanksgiving with intention we can move up the emotional scale making anger much less likely.

The emotion of gratitude is very powerful. When we work from a disposition of thanks and gratitude it makes it easy for us to be both giving and to see opportunity.

The opposite of gratitude is poverty. When I say poverty I don't just mean in terms of not having money. The emotion of poverty is the emotion of scarcity or lack. It could be lack of work, money, opportunity, love, or recognition.

When we think about the posture of gratitude it is an open posture. I imagine gratitude as standing up straight with my arms spread wide. I am open to everything the world has for me. The posture of poverty is just the opposite. When I think of poverty I imagine being curled up in a tight ball clinging to what little I have. It is impossible to pick up anything new because I am afraid I might lose what little I have.

When we are working from a position of gratitude it is possible for us to see new opportunities. I would like to be clear that I am not talking about a blind sense of "everything is going to just work out great." It is possible to look at our lives with honesty, warts and all, and still be able to feel gratitude. I know my life is far from perfect but even when things have been at their worst there were things for which I could be thankful.

When we are able to tune into that sense of gratitude then we can start to move in a more positive direction. We can recognize that we can continue to move forward in a positive way even when things around us are not perfect.

I do this exercise most mornings to start my day off on the right foot.

1) Come up with a list of 10 things you are thankful for

These things can be as big as the birth of your children or a letter from a loved one. Add the ten things to the list below. If you are doing the work on a separate sheet of paper (which I recommend) copy all the letters and the lines that are listed between them.

[See worksheet on next page]

A)

B)

Thank you for the blessings I have received and the blessings I am receiving.

C)

D)

Thank you! Thank you! Thank you!

E)

F)

Thank you for the blessings I have received and the blessings I am receiving.

G)

H)

Thank you! Thank you! Thank you!

I)

J)

Thank you for the blessings I have received and the blessings I am receiving.

2) Tap though the above list

Take a deep breath and start to tap, moving to a new tapping point with each new line as you read it out loud, including the lines that are inserted between those you have written. Tap through the list three times.

Note: This is one of those exercises where it is easy just to go through the motions. Saying the words out loud alone does not mean that you are engaged with what you are doing. For tapping to have any effect we must be tuned in emotionally. As you read each of the lines think about what you are saying, why you appreciate these things and what you get from them. Don't just say thank you, but feel gratitude.

Beliefs Given To Us By Others

What we believe about the world is shaped by our experience. Not only do we learn from what directly happens to us, but we also learn from what the people closest to us believe, particularly our parents. It makes perfect sense that we pick up the patterns, traits, and beliefs of our parents. They are the ones who cared for us and taught us during our most formative years and culturally we grow up to believe that they care for us more than anyone else. Not all of these patterns and beliefs are helpful.

As children we tend to believe that if our parents say something is true, then it must be true. But as adults we can see clearly that our parents are far from perfect. Many of the thoughts, beliefs, and habits that our parents had don't feel right for us. They might be outdated or just plain wrong, like "men shouldn't show emotions". When we pick up these types of beliefs from our parents (or anyone who is important to us) it can be difficult to let them go.

When we let these beliefs go it can feel like we are also dismissing, letting go, or disrespecting the people who gave us these beliefs. Our subconscious could tell us:

- If I let go of this I am saying I don't love my mother
- If I let go of this I am saying that I am letting go of my father
- If I let go of this I am saying that my mother was wrong
- If I let go of this I am saying that my father is not worth anything to me

Even though none of these thoughts is grounded in truth, if the subconscious believes them to be true then it will be difficult to transform these beliefs.

For example, as you have worked through the tools in this book you more than likely came across some things that brought up a lot of emotions from the past. If you think that "real men don't show their emotions" it will be hard to find the time to use the tools in this book because your system will see it as unsafe. Part of you understands that if you use these tools you will feel emotional, you shouldn't feel emotions, therefore you will not do the work.

This will lead to you not making the progress required to heal. Here is a simple process to help to let go of the thoughts, beliefs, and traits we have been given by loved ones without feeling like we are disrespecting or letting our loved ones go. The first time you do this process I recommend that you do it for three different beliefs.

Here is a list of sample beliefs to get you thinking in the right way:

- Real men don't show their emotions.
- Asking for help is a sign of weakness.
- Rich people are mean and selfish.
- You have to work hard to get ahead.
- The men in our family are no good with relationships.
- The women in our family aren't good at math.

1) Naming The Belief And Who Gave It To You
Name a belief that you were given by a loved one and who that person was.

The belief I was given that I know isn't true is...

It was given to me by...

2) Name The Reason For The Belief
There is a reason that our loved ones believe what they do. It could be a belief they were given by their parents. It could that they were were dealing with their own baggage and didn't know any other way. For example, you father might have been uncomfortable dealing with his emotions so he adopted the belief that "real men don't show their emotions" as an excuse to avoid his own emotions. When you are coming up with the reasons why they held a belief you will be guessing. That is OK. Come up with two or three possibilities for why they might have held that belief.

The reason they had this belief is...

3) Naming The Belief You Would Like Instead
It is good that you are able to name what you no longer want. It is just as important that you name the new belief you would like instead.

The belief that I want to have and know is true is...

The reason I want this new belief is...

4) Tap Through The Script
Take a deep breath. Start tapping. Tap through all the notes you have written above. When you come to a new sentence move on to the next tapping point. Once you have tapped through all of your notes tap through the script below.

I know that I am approaching this just like the people in my life...and I know that approach is not serving me...but there is a part of me that doesn't want to let this belief go...there is a part of me that believes that if I let this belief go then I am letting them go...that I am saying that they are wrong...I am saying that I don't love them...I am saying that I am not grateful for what they have done for me...but I know this is not true...I can let go beliefs that they had without letting go of them...I can know that I love them and that they love me and not hold everything they said or did as true...They were imperfect...and it is OK to say that they were and are imperfect...and there are many beliefs that served them in a time and place that don't serve me...they want what is best for me...and they might think that one way is right...but even when they want things for me that aren't perfect for me...they do this because they want what is best for me...I can do what is best for me and love my parents...I can do what is best for me and appreciate everything they have done for me...I can do what is best for me and keep the relationship strong...letting go of something they have given me is not the same as letting them go.

Transform Your Critical Voice In 8 Steps

One of the reasons that I love tapping is because it is very effective in dealing with our critical voice. The critical voice is nothing more than that little nagging voice in our head that is always pointing out everything we have done wrong, everything we are going to do wrong, and everything we will never be.

Sometimes this voice is nothing more than a simple annoyance, while at other times it can be so crippling that it prevents us from getting out of bed in the morning. When our critical voice is nagging away it is easy for us to be on the edge of anger at any given moment.

Because of this most of us don't have a good relationship with our critical voice. Many of us resent it and even hate it. There are guys in class who have said that one of the main reasons they drank or smoked pot so much was to numb or quiet the critical voice.

It is difficult for us to transform our critical voice when we are angry at it. When we are angry at a part of our personality it will entrench itself and fight back. If we are willing to change our attitude toward this part of our personality then we can get it to work with us to create lasting and deep transformation.

Before we can begin the process we need to understand why the critical voice exists.

And the reason might surprise you.

The Critical Voice Exists To Make Your Life Better

I know that statement is extremely hard to believe. I would even be willing to bet that when you read that statement there was a strong emotional reaction against it, but it's true.

All parts of our personality exist because they are trying to bring us to our higher good. Just because a part's motivation is for higher good does NOT mean that it is leading us to our higher good. In this example the critical voice is not pointing things out to make us feel bad or to punish us, but instead is doing so to help us see the errors of our ways so that we will make better choices in the future.

And yes, I know it doesn't feel that way. It feels like it is just judging and criticizing.

But, when we are able to recognize that it is trying to help us, it will make it easier for us to transform it into something that is truly helpful. As you will see in this process we do not need to celebrate what the critical voice has done to us to recognize its motivation.

The Process For Transforming Your Critical Voice With Tapping & EFT

Even if you don't buy my "The critical voice is here to help you, but is just doing it in the wrong way", I would encourage you to give this process a try. If it doesn't work out for you then go back to being mad at the critical voice. The only thing you will have lost is a few minutes tapping on something new.

1) Tune in and connect with the critical voice

In this step all we need to do is connect with the critical voice. Just close your eyes, take a deep breath, and listen for the voice. It will not be hard to find. Pay attention to where the voice is coming from.

- Is it something that is internal or external?
- Is it the voice of someone you know, does it sound like your speaking voice, or is it some other voice?
- If you were to imagine that the voice belonged to a body, what would that body look like?

The specific answers to these questions aren't important, but by asking them it will be easier for us to connect with the critical part of ourselves, allowing us to do healing work.

2) Affirm the critical voice

This is going to be the most difficult step of the process because of the hurt and harm we associate with the critical voice. It is important to note that when doing this step we are NOT affirming the tactics of the critical voice and we are NOT affirming the way we feel after we encounter our critical voice. What we are affirming is that it is a part of us that is willing to work very hard to move us to a better life. To do this we would tap on something like:

> *I would like to give thanks for my critical voice…I am NOT thankful for the tactic that it is using…I am NOT thankful for the way I feel after I experience the critical voice…I am thankful for the fact that there is a part of me that is willing to work so hard…I know that even though it is not doing this…it is trying to make my life better…my critical voice thinks it is making my life better…it thinks that if it berates me…or if it points out everything that is going wrong…that it is going make me make better choices in the future…the critical voice is a very powerful part of me…even if it is not working in a productive way…I know it is working for my betterment…I am thankful that there is a part of me that is willing to work day and night…thinking it is doing what is best for me.*

After doing a round of tapping like this we will take some of the edge off. We might not be super-happy with the critical voice, but there is less animosity towards it. At this point that is all we are trying to achieve. When we move from a state of animosity then we are no longer fighting a part of ourselves, and we can now start to work with it.

3) Explain to the critical voice what it is really doing

As stated above the critical voice in most cases believes that if it is constantly pointing out every flaw and fault, it will motivate us to make better choices. Its motives are either "You don't know you are doing something wrong?" and/or "You don't realize the consequences of these choices?"

In almost every case we are fully aware of the information that the critical voice is providing. In many cases the critical voice is actually over-stating and/or overreacting to the situation around us. Because we have taken the last step and created a bit of a truce with the critical voice, we can now speak to it with new information.

In this step we are simply going let the critical voice know the consequences of its actions. Try tapping like this:

> *I know the critical voice is trying to be helpful…but it isn't…the critical voice is pointing out things I already know…and many times is it pointing out things in a way that is much worse that it really is…the critical voice thinks it is going to encourage me by pointing out my failings…instead I find having every flaw and failing being pointed out to be disheartening…debilitating…I find it very hurtful…I find that it makes it extremely difficult to believe in myself…it is not pushing me to be better…but instead it is sucking my ability to try right out of my system…I know the critical voice believes it is being helpful…it is not…it is not creating a feeling of encouragement for better…it is creating a feeling of shame…shame is not an emotion of achievement and growth…shame is a feeling of not wanting to try.*

4) Show the critical voice proof of its past tactics

At this point it is helpful to show the critical voice the proof of what we have just been tapping on. Again, just tune into the critical voice, begin to tap from point to point, and show the critical voice proof of all the ways it has been hurtful and debilitating.

5) Transforming the critical voice into something helpful

When doing the process with clients there is something very interesting that happens. Clients describe the fact that they can feel the critical voice feeling bad that it has not done its job. I have even had clients describe their critical voice as feeling bad because it feels it is about to be eliminated from the system.

Because we are not fighting with the critical voice (like we were in the beginning), but instead have a relationship with it, we can now guide it to a resource that is helpful. The tapping for this transformation might look like this:

> *I know the critical voice is very powerful…I have felt the force of its power…but instead of pointing out all of the things I have done wrong…there is a way this voice can be more helpful…I want to harness the power of the voice to be used for my higher good…because I know this voice wants my higher good…I want this voice to stop being a critical voice and become an encouraging voice…because I respond so much better to encouragement…I want this encouraging voice to pick me up when I am down…I want this encouraging voice to push me on to take those last few hard steps…I want the encouraging voice to help me to get started when I can't quite focus on the task at hand…I want the encouraging voice to use the power it had to see my faults in the past to start to look forward to the opportunities in my future…I want this encouraging voice to move me forward…not keep me stuck in the past…when it does this I will move forward and heal.*

This is a very empowering step.

6) Giving the encouraging voice the resources and tools to do its new job

Just because we want the voice to change (and just because the critical voice wants to become the encouraging voice) doesn't mean the change is going to happen. I have had many clients describe the feeling of having the critical voice being on board with the change but not know what to do next.

I have found the easiest way to complete the change is to ask the critical/encouraging voice what it needs for transformation. The process for this is simple. First, start tapping from point to point. Second, tune back into the critical/encouraging voice. Third, ask it one of the following questions. Fourth, if it states a need based on the questions simply imagine that need being fulfilled.

For example, if it needs permission to change, give it permission. If it needs to know how to encourage you, show it.

Here is a list of sample questions you can ask the voice to help it transform from critical to encouraging.

- Do you need permission to transform?
- Do you need training to transform? If so what type?
- Do you energy to transform? If so what type?

- Do you need to be connected to other parts of the system? What type of connections need to be made?
- What do you need from me to make the transformation?

7) Reassure the encouraging voice

Even when we choose to make this type of transformation it doesn't always take place all at once. And that is OK. The transformation process can take time. We want the healing to happen in a fashion that is long lasting. We are not looking for a short-term quick fix.

The last part of the process is to reassure the encouraging voice that this will take time and that we are willing to help it through the transformation.

Try tapping like this:

> *I am very happy that my internal voice is willing to become an encouraging voice...I know this process is going to take a little time...which is OK because I want lasting change...not a quick fix...I want my encouraging voice to know that I don't expect it to be perfect right way...I know it is going to need to learn its way into this new role...I commit to check in regularly with the encouraging voice...making sure it has everything it needs to complete this transformation...I give the encouraging voice permission to ask for help from me...even when I am not checking in with it...this is a change that is good for me now...and for the future.*

8) Check back regularly

If this is a process that is helpful for you I would encourage you to do it two or three times a month for a few months to help this transformation process along. I think it is obvious how making the small change of changing one aspect of our personality will cascade into many radical changes in our lives.

What Others Say About Us

It can be hard when other people are talking about us. Sometimes they are telling stories about our past that we don't want others to know about, or they may be saying things about us that aren't true and affect how other people see us.

As we have seen many times before, we can't control what others do. When someone is doing something as hurtful as telling lies about us it can be really hard to confront the person who is saying those things in a calm and measured way.

Here is a simple tool you can use to control your anger and respond reasonably when someone is talking negatively about you.

1) Answer the following questions in as much detail as possible

For this concentrate on one person or one instance when people were saying something about you that you didn't like. This process will be more effective the more specific you are and you can use it as many times as you need to.

A) Who is saying bad things about you?

_____ *is saying bad things about me.*

B) What are they saying about you?

They have said...

C) Why is it bad that they are saying these things? How does it hurt you or others when they say it?

When they say this it hurts me by...

When they say this it hurts others by...

D) What is untrue in what they are saying?

The untrue things they are saying are...

E) What is really true about the situation?

The truth of the matter is...

F) Why would they be saying this? When you answer this question you will be guessing, but what are some of the reasons that they might be saying this about you?

If I were to guess, the reason they are saying this is because...

G) What does this situation remind you of? Often when people are saying bad things about us it reminds us of other times when we were not treated well and because of this the current situation can feel much worse.

> *In some ways this reminds me of the time when...*

H) Who does this situation remind you of? Often when people say untrue things about us it reminds us of a previous time when someone hurt us and because it is something that is happening again, it feels worse.

> *In some ways this reminds me of...*

2) Tap through your answers

Take a nice deep breath and tap your way through what you have written down. Each time you start a new sentence move on to the next tapping point. Tap through what you have written three times.

As you are tapping it is possible that more information will come to mind. If this happens, stop, add the new information to the page, and then continue tapping.

3) Tune back into the situation

After tapping through the questions three times check how you now feel about the situation. If there is still an emotional charge around what has been said about you tap through the answers a few more times.

Remember that when we do this kind of tapping we are not trying to get to the point where we don't care about what others are saying about us. What we are trying to do is get to a place where we are not overcome with emotion and anger to the point that we respond in a poor way. It is important that we stand up for ourselves. It is important that we set the record straight, but we want to respond calmly and thoughtfully.

It is entirely possible that some of the things that we tap for in this exercise will not require a response. After tapping we may realize that the person who is talking about us has no power or influence and it doesn't matter what they say about us. Other times we will realize that we need to say or do something to stop it, but after we tap for it we will respond much more calmly.

Wanting Better For Others

As we explored in a previous section (About, To, As If, and Surrogate Tapping) we can't change the choices that other people make. What we can control is how we respond emotionally to the people in our lives and the space that we create for them.

It can be really tough when we see the people we love making choices that hurt themselves, hurt others, and hurt us. When we are experiencing these types of emotions we are likely to be that much closer to being angry at others for their choices, or angry at ourselves for not being able to control what is going on.

This tool is great to use when there is someone in your life for whom you want better, but they can't seem to make better choices.

1) Answer the following questions in as much detail as possible

If there is more than one person involved in a situation, such as you want better for your daughter and her husband, do this process twice. Once for each of them.

A) Whose life do you want to see better?

I would like _____ to have a better life and an easier time.

B) Describe their struggle in detail. Include how you believe their choices are hurting them and how they are hurting others.

The struggle they are facing is...

C) Describe in as much detail as possible the emotions you feel about the situation. This could include how you are being hurt, as well as any other emotions you are feeling such as overwhelmed, frustrated, sad, etc.

As I see this happening I feel...

D) Describe the secondary gains or benefits they could be receiving from this situation. When we are coming up with secondary gains we are guessing, so just make your best guess. (For a refresher on secondary gains see the section titled "Secondary Gain".)

The possible secondary gains they are receiving from this are...

E) Describe the truth of the situation as you see it. Often we when have loved ones who are making poor choices or going through a hard time it is because they are deluding themselves over what is truly going on. How do you see the situation from the outside?

What I see is really going on is...

F) Describe what better outcome you would want for them. This might include them being in a different situation, making different choices, and/or seeing themselves differently. Often when loved ones struggle it is because they think so little of themselves and it is wonderful for us to want them to understand that they are good and lovable.

What I want for them is...

G) Describe how they would benefit from this better outcome. Often when someone's life gets better there is more to it than just the change that happens. If someone leaves a relationship with an abusive partner, not only will they be safer, but they will also find peace, sleep better, have opportunities to grow, etc.

What they would get from this change is...

H) Describe how you would benefit if their life were better. It is OK to name the ways our lives would be better if the lives of others improve. For example, if a loved one was able to stay sober we wouldn't dread hearing the phone ring in the early hours, knowing that we had to bail them out. You might have improved peace of mind, more sleep, or just the joy of knowing your loved one is living a better life.

How I would benefit if their life improved is...

I) Describe what you can do for them today. Even though we can't change the choices that others make and we can't take on their burdens, there are things that we can do for them today. It might be as simple as calling them to tell them we love them, saying a prayer for them, or doing something small for them.

The things I can do for them right now are...

2) Tap through the script you have just written

Take a deep breath and start at the beginning and read out loud everything you have written. As you get to a new sentence move to the next tapping point. If new information and ideas come to mind for one of the answers as you are moving through the script, stop tapping and add the information to the sheet. Tap through the entire script three times.

What I Choose For Today

Part of transforming the way we act is by knowing exactly what we want. When we name what we want it helps us to get through the places that are hard for us because we have already identified what will do instead. It is much like practicing a fire drill. By practicing what you are supposed to do in the event of a fire you will be ready when it happens .

This tool is a perfect way to start your day. Not only will it set you up to avoid angry responses, it will also move you towards what you do want. There are five places below to name exactly what you want for different areas of your life. Take the time to fill those in before you tap. Once you have added all the details you can tap through the whole script.

Today for my physical body I want to be healthy...

I want to know the joy of my body...

I want to appreciate all the things my body does...

I want to appreciate that my body does so many things I don't know about...

I want my body to continue to heal...

I also want *(write two more things you want for your body today)...*

Today for my relationships I want to recognize the ways they feed me...

I want to grow closer to someone I love...

I want to support someone in need...

I want to have the courage to ask for help from someone else...

I want to learn something new from a friend...

I want to learn what it means to be a better friend...

I want to learn what friendship does for me...

I also want *(write two more things you want from your friendships today)...*

Today from my work and activities I want to spend time doing something I love...

I want to get better at one thing...

Even if it is just in a small way...

I want to recognize the ways in which I am growing and getting better at something...

I want to be able to teach someone else something I have learned...

I also want *(write two more things you want for your activities and work today)...*

Today from my spiritual journey I want to know more deeply who I am...

I want to recognize the hand of God in my day...

I want to have the opportunity for my spirit to grow...

I want to be a model for others to grow in faith and spirit...

I want to recognize how I have grown...

I want to see a new path for growth and transformation...

Even if it is with something small...

I also want *(write two more things you want for your spiritual self today)...*

Today for my emotional self I want to know that I am in control...

I want to be able to feel my emotions without feeling compelled to act on them...

I want to know what information these emotions are conveying...

I want to hear these emotions and let them go...

I want to know that emotions are not the enemy...

I want to know that feeling emotions doesn't mean I have failed...

I want my emotions to show up when they are useful...

I want my emotions to show up today at a level that is right for the situation...

I want them to not be too little or too much..

I also want (write two more things you want for your emotional self today)...

Journaling

There have been a number studies that have shown that the simple act of journaling is a healthy way to help reduce the amount of emotion and stress that build up inside us. Many of the tools in this book give you the opportunity to get things out of your head in a structured way so that you can let them go, gain extra perspective on them, and move towards healing.

When I talk about journaling I am not talking about getting a pink notebook that says "My Diary" on the front (with the i on diary dotted with a heart). There are times when we don't feel like answering questions or tuning into something specific. There is just a bunch of stuff that gets you and journaling by writing or typing is a direct and easy way to get it out of your head.

AND (most importantly) you don't need to keep what you have written. The goal of the exercise isn't to keep a record of what you are thinking. It is to get it out of your head. You take 15 minutes to write and when you are done you can tear the paper up and throw it away or delete the file on the computer. For me, it just feels good to rip up the paper after I have written down whatever is going around in my head.

The journaling exercise:

1) Journal

Get a piece of paper or open a blank document on your computer and just start writing. Let it all out. Write about what is going on, write down what you are thinking, what you feel, and about the things that are worrying you. Don't edit. Don't go back and re-read. Don't worry about grammar and spelling. Just keep writing. Even if you don't know what to write, keep writing.

2) Tap

After you have written for a set amount of time, like 15 minutes, or you have run out of steam, take a few minutes to tap. You can choose one of the tapping scripts from the back of this book or you can just re-read what you wrote and tap along to it.

3) Get rid of it!

Delete the file. Tear up the piece of paper. Just get rid of it. You will feel better for it.

Chapter 6 – Now What?

Anger Management Post-Test

Now that you have worked your way through all of the tools take a few minutes to take the post-test. This is an opportunity to see the amount of progress you have made now that you have completed the book.

When doing a post-test like this it is tempting to answer the questions in a way that shows you in a positive light. It is important that you fill this out as honestly as you are able. Taking this post-test isn't just to make you feel good because your score is now lower, it is designed to show how much progress you have made.

Just because you have completed the tools and activities in this book does not mean that your work is finished. It means that you have made progress and that there is still work to be done. Use the test honestly to see what has improved and what still needs work.

3 for "often"; 2 for "some of the time"; 1 for "rarely"; 0 for "never"

_____ I think that other people cause me to be angry.

_____ When someone disagrees with me, I work hard to make sure they know that they're wrong.

_____ When I think about something that bothered me in the past, I can get very angry about it all over again.

_____ I think that people who make mistakes should be reprimanded and clearly told they did something wrong.

_____ I feel impatient when I have to wait in a line.

_____ When I am around people I don't like, I let them know one way or another.

_____ When I see someone who is overweight, I start to think about how little self-discipline he or she has.

_____ When I get really angry I throw, hit, or break things.

_____ I get angry if things don't go the way I want them to go.

_____ When something does not go my way, I progress from having no anger to experiencing rage and aggression in seconds.

_____ I get really upset with myself when I make a mistake or don't do something well.

_____ When someone treats me badly, I start to think about ways to get even with them.

_____ If I'm really mad at other people, I'm likely to put them down and swear at them.

_____ I generally believe that people would be dishonest if they could actually get away with it.

_____ My anger overwhelms me at times and I seem to lose control.

_____ If someone hurts or offends me, I end up thinking about it a lot and have a hard time letting it go.

_____ When I get angry I've experienced chest pain, headaches, or other physical symptoms.

_____ When I have something important to say I want to jump in and interrupt other people, rather than listen.

_____ Other people tell me they are worried and tell me about what happens when I get angry or how often I get mad.

_____ I don't like how I act when I get angry and I end up feeling bad about what I said   or did.

_____ I think I have a "thin skin" and am easily affected by what others say and do.

(Adapted from Tracey Middleton's adaptation of work of David J. Decker, MA, LP.)

___ Total up score
___ Look up score from pre-test

Now What?

You have worked your way through the book. You have completed all the activities. You have even taken the post-test and recognize that things are getting better. So now what?

When it comes to managing our anger it is a process that will take more time than just working through the exercises in this book. As powerful as the exercises are, doing them just once isn't enough.

I want you to flip back to the goals you wrote for yourself back in section 2A "When We Start." I am willing to bet you are closer to these goals than you were when we started, but you haven't made it there yet.

The goal of this book wasn't to complete the exercises. The goal of this book is for you to have those things you named as your goals.

There is still work to be done.

28 Days To More Control

A simple way to make sure you continue to make progress is to set aside a little time every day to keep working toward your goals. One of the reasons these tools are presented in small bite-sized chunks is so that you can easily go back to them again and again.

The next step is to make a commitment that for the next four weeks you will do one of the tools in this book every single day. Most of them are straightforward and take less than seven minutes to complete.

One word of caution: it will be extremely tempting to keep going back to the tools you find easiest. If you find a tool easy to do, more than likely it isn't having a high impact. If there are tools that you dread doing, more than likely those are the exact tools you need to be doing because that is where you need the most work.

Be easy with yourself. You don't have to do any of the tools or exercises perfectly. If you keep after it and do a little every day it will make a huge difference.

Appendix

Other Resources

TappingQandA.com

As of the publication of this book there are over 500 free articles, tapping scripts, tap-along audios, and interviews with some of the brightest minds in the EFT world. Every week at least two new resources are added.

TappingQandAPodcast.com

This is the podcast sister site of TappingQandA.com. As of the publication of this book there are over 130 interviews and teachings, all available free of charge.

Emofree.com

This is the website of Gary Craig, the original innovator of EFT. This work would not exist without his work and dedication.

EFTUniverse.com

On this site you will find thousands of articles written by practitioners and lay users of tapping from all over the world on hundreds of topics.

Made in the USA
Charleston, SC
16 April 2013